BMA's

TALENT & OLYMPIAD

EXAMS RESOURCE BOOK

CLASS VIII

Science

BRAIN MAPPING
A C A D E M Y
Mapping Your Future

www.bmatalent.com

Published by:

Brain Mapping Academy

#16–11–16/1/B, First Floor, Farhath Hospital Road,
Saleem Nagar, Malakpet, Hyderabad–500 036.
© 040–66135169,65165169.
E–mail: info@bmatalent.com
Website: www.bmatalent.com

ISBN : 978-93-82058-62-5

Disclaimer

Every care has been taken by the compilers and
publishers to give correct, complete and updated information.
In case there is any omission, printing mistake or any
other error which might have crept in inadvertently,
neither the compiler / publisher nor any of the
distributors take any legal responsibility.

*In case of any dispute, all matters are subjected to the exclusive
jurisdiction of the courts in Hyderabad only.*

First Edition   : 2003
Second Edition   : 2008
Revised Edition : 2015

Printed at:
Sri Vinayaka Art Printers, Hyderabad.

Publisher's Note

Sometimes the understanding of fundamental concepts alone does not help the students to crack the competitive exams as most of them are objective in structure. Students need rigorous training to familiarize themselves to the style of the exams they are attempting. The board exams which are of qualifying, but not competitive, nature do not completely address the needs of students in testing them in objective type format.

To bridge this gap and to enable the students to face the reality of competitive exams, Brain Mapping Academy, brought out an all-objective questions reference book.

A crisp summary of the topics and useful equations were provided at the beginning of each chapter so that the students can memorize the important points.

Care has been taken to design thought-provoking questions. These should help students to attain a deeper understanding of principles. The questions have been reviewed to fill the gaps in problem coverage and to build the confidence in the students. They have also been expanded to impart reasoning/logical/analytical skills.

This book will cater all the requirements of the students who are approaching national/state level talent search examinations and all Olympiad exams. This book also complements the additional preparation needs of the students for the regular board exams.

We took utmost care to make this the best resource book available for the Talent & Olympiad exams aspirants. We welcome criticism from the students, teacher community and educators, especially concerning any errors and deficiencies which may have remained in this edition and the suggestions for improvement for the next edition.

NATIONAL LEVEL SCIENCE TALENT SEARCH EXAMINATION

Aim of this examination

The focus on fundamentals is so important that without a firm understanding of them, a child cannot be expected to face the reality of the competitive world once he/she finishes the formal education. Even while opting for higher studies the student has to go through a complete scan of what he/she knows. Exams like IIT-JEE, AIEEE, AIIMS, AFMC, CAT, SAT, GRE, GMAT, etc. are so designed to test the fundamental strength of a student. Hence the need of the hour is building the fundamental base as strong as possible.

A successful life emerges out from healthy and sound competition. Competition is the only way for the students to shake lethargy. It's the only way to get introduced for manly worthiness. Firm standards in education and competition are the tonic for a promising and talented future.

This exactly is the philosophy behind the Unified Council's NSTSE.

Organisation

National Science Talent Search Examination is conducted by Unified Council. Unified Council is India's first ISO 9001 certified organisation in the educational testing and assessment. Since its inception, Unified Council has put together the best brains in an endeavour to make the younger generation fundamentally stronger and nourish their brains for a bright and enterprising future.

Eligibility : Students of classes 1, 2, 3, 4, 5, 6, 7, 8, 9, 10, 11 & 12 are eligible to participate in this examination.

Medium & Syllabus: This exam is conducted in only English medium and is suitable for all the students following CBSE/ICSE/State Board Syllabi.

Examination Pattern

There will be a separate question paper for each class. All questions are objective-type multiple-choice with no negative marking for wrong answers.

Duration: 90 minutes

Date : Conducted every year on the last Sunday of January.

Test Centres : Spread across the country.

DIVISION OF MARKS

FOR CLASS I			FOR CLASSES VI TO X		
Mathematics	:	25 marks	Mathematics	:	25 marks
General Science	:	15 Marks	Physics	:	25 marks
FOR CLASS II			Chemistry	:	20 marks
			Biology	:	20 marks
Mathematics	:	25 marks	General Questions	:	10 marks
General Science	:	25 Marks	**FOR CLASS XI & XII(PCM)**		
FOR CLASS III			Mathematics	:	40 marks
			Physics	:	25 marks
Mathematics	:	40 marks	Chemistry	:	25 marks
General Science	:	35 Marks	General Questions	:	10 marks
FOR CLASSES IV & V			**FOR CLASS XI & XII(PCB)**		
			Biology	:	40 marks
Mathematics	:	45 marks	Physics	:	25 marks
General Science	:	45 Marks	Chemistry	:	25 marks
General Questions	:	10 marks	General Questions	:	10 marks

Infrastructure

The Council makes use of ultra-modern equipment such as **Optical Mark Recognition (OMR)** equipment to evaluate the answer papers to proficiently assess students' performance. The examination procedure is **completely computerised.**

Unique Service from Unified Council:

Unique analysis reports like Student's Performance Report for students, General School Report & Individual School Report for schools provided. These reports are very much helpful for students & schools to analyse their strengths and weaknesses.

General School Report (GSR) analyses the performance of students participating in the exam (subject-wise and class-wise). The report, in graphical format will have Ogive and Histogram Graphs, which are useful to schools that wish to improve their students' performance by benchmarking the areas of weaknesses and building upon them.

Individual School Report (ISR) analyses the performance of a particular school when compared to the rest of the students participating in this examination (subject-wise, class-wise and question-wise). This report acts as a tool for the schools to improve their students' performance in the future by benchmarking the areas of weaknesses and building upon them.

Awards & Scholarships:

Top 100 members in each class will be awarded with Awards & Medals etc.

UNIFIED COUNCIL
An ISO 9001: 2008 Certified Organisation
Foundation for success

#16-11-16/1/B, Farhath Hospital Road, Saleem Nagar, Malakpet, Hyderabad-500 036
Phones : 040-24557708, 24545862, 66139917
E-mail: exam@unifiedcouncil.com, Website: www.unifiedcouncil.com

CONTENTS

Physics

Chemistry

Biology

CONTENTS

Force and Pressure

- A force is a push or a pull. It can cause any one, two or all of the following when applied to a body:
    - (a)   cause movement or stop motion of an object
    - (b)   change its speed/direction of the motion of a body
    - (c)   change its shape and size of a body
- Forces that are in contact with a body are muscular force, frictional force.
    Forces that are not in contact with a body and act from a distance are magnetic force, electrostatic force, gravitational force.
- Force is due to the interaction between two or more bodies.
- The strength of a force is expressed by its magnitude and is a vector quantity.
- Net force on an object can be zero if two (or more) forces acting on it in opposite directions are equal in magnitude.
- Frictional force is responsible for change of speed of an object. It tends to stop/slow down a moving object in the absence of external forces. Frictional force can be due to a surface, wind (drag) or water (ex. a moving boat stops in water if you stop rowing).
- Force acting on a unit area of a surface is called pressure. Pressure = Force/Area on which it acts.

> **Note :** S.I. unit of force = newton
> S.I. unit of pressure = newton $(metre)^{-2}$ or pascal

- Pressure depends upon the area of contact.
    Ex. : A sharp needle causes more pain in the body as compared to a blunt object.
- Pressure exerted by water at the bottom of a container depends upon the height of the water column.
- Both liquids and gases exert pressure on the walls of a container in which they are stored.
- Liquids exert equal pressure at the same depth.
- Pressure exerted by the air surrounding the earth is called the atmospheric pressure. The reason we do not feel this pressure is due to the fact that the pressure inside our bodies (Our blood contains dissolved oxygen at a pressure, equal to or slightly more than the atmospheric pressure) is equal to the atmospheric pressure and hence, cancels the pressure from outside.
    Atmospheric pressure is measured in Pascals or kilopascals.
    1 atmosphere (1 atm) = 101325 Pa or 101.325 k Pa.
- Atmospheric pressure decreases with height (high altitude/mountains) and increases with depth (deep sea).

Multiple Choice Questions   (A) (B) (C) (D)

1 Which of the following actions describe pushing force?

(A) Kicking   (B) Lifting
(C) Picking   (D) Opening

2 Which of the following is NOT a force?

(A) Muscular   (B) Magnetic
(C) Chemical   (D) Electric

3 A force is applied on an object in the direction of its motion. What is the effect of force on the object?

(A) The speed of the object will increase.
(B) The speed of the object will decrease.
(C) The speed of the object will remain unchanged.
(D) The object comes to rest.

4 If no force acts on a body at rest, then what effect can be observed?

(A) The body changes shape.
(B) The body moves with increased speed.
(C) The body remains at rest.
(D) The body breaks up.

5 Which of the following examples describe the change of shape on applying force?

(A) A ball being kicked
(B) A fan switched on
(C) A man jumping from a height
(D) Repeatedly tearing of a paper

6 Which of the following effects is caused by frictional force?

(A) Change in the shape of an object
(B) Change in the direction of the motion of an object
(C) Slowing down of a moving object
(D) Acceleration in a moving body

7 Which of the following is a non-contact force?

(A) Muscular force
(B) Electrostatic force
(C) Elastic spring force
(D) Frictional force

8 What causes the atmospheric pressure?

(A) The sky above our head
(B) The air surrounding the earth
(C) The gravitational force of the sun and other planets
(D) The mass of the earth

9 How does the pressure exerted by a liquid change?

(A) Increases with depth
(B) Decreases with depth
(C) Remains constant
(D) First increases and then decreases

10 What is thrust equal to?

(A) Force × area   (B) Force/area
(C) Pressure   (D) Pressure × area

11 When does a body float on water?

(A) When no force is acting on it.
(B) When the net force acting on the body is zero
(C) When there is a gravitational pull.
(D) When there is friction between the body and the water

12 In which of the following cases the net force is NOT equal to zero?

(A) A kite held stationary in the sky.
(B) A ball falling freely from a height.
(C) A helicopter hovering above the ground.
(D) A cork floating on the surface of water.

13 We use a straw (narrow pipe) to drink juice from a glass. What make this possible?

(A) The volume of liquid
(B) The atmospheric pressure
(C) The gravitational pull
(D) All of the above

14 Which of the following effects is NOT caused by the magnetic force between a magnet and a magnetic substance?

(A) Change of state
(B) Change of shape
(C) Change of size
(D) Change of chemical composition

15 In cities, water from an overhead tank is supplied to houses using the principle of

(i) difference in pressure.
(ii) gravitational force.
(iii) decrease of friction in pipes.

(A) Only (i)   (B) Only (i) and (ii)
(C) Only (ii) and (iii) (D) (i), (ii) and (iii)

16 A deep sea diver's ears get hurt when he is inside the water. What is the cause for it?

(A) Lack of oxygen
(B) Decrease in atmospheric pressure
(C) Increase in water pressure
(D) All of the above

17 What does a barometer measure?

(A) Liquid pressure
(B) Thrust
(C) Atmospheric pressure
(D) Air temperature

18 Four forces are acting on a body. If the body does not change its position or shape, then what does it mean?

(A) Forces are similar acting in the same direction.
(B) Forces are parallel and opposite.
(C) Forces add up to zero when taken as vectors.
(D) Forces are different acting in the same direction.

19 Why do deep sea divers use a special suit for diving?

(A) To maintain their body temperature in cold sea water
(B) To protect against sea animals
(C) To counter balance the pressure in the sea.
(D) To keep them dry

20 On what factors does the magnitude of non-contact force depend?

(A) Distance between two bodies
(B) Mass of the two bodies
(C) Chemical composition of the two bodies
(D) All of the above

21 Why does a rubber sucker stick to a surface?

(A) It is the inherent property of rubber.
(B) Gravitational force acts on it.
(C) Elastic spring force acts on it.
(D) Atmospheric pressure acts on it.

22 Which force does an archer use to pull a bow?

(A) Muscular force
(B) Magnetic force
(C) Gravitational force
(D) All of the above

23 A player slides a bowling ball on the lane to hit the pins. What is the effect of the force exerted on the bowling ball ?

(A) Stops the moving bowling ball
(B) Changes the direction of the moving bowling ball
(C) Changes the shape of the moving bowling ball
(D) Changes the position of the stationary pins

24 Which of the following requires a pushing force?

(A) Throwing a stone
(B) Grabbing hold of a pencil
(C) Leaves falling from a tree
(D) A load lifted by a pulley

25 Identify the application of low pressure in everyday life.

(A) Wide tyres of a heavy vehicle
(B) Cutting of an apple with a sharp knife
(C) Hammering of a nail into wood
(D) All of the above

Previous Contest Questions

1 Which of the following does NOT require a force?

(A) Rowing of a boat
(B) Bursting of a balloon filled with lots of air.
(C) Pedalling a cycle
(D) Catching a moving cricket ball

2 Which of the following is true of the man in the picture shown below?

(A) He is applying force on the stool.
(B) He represents only magnitude but no direction.
(C) He is not applying any force on the stool.
(D) The gravitational pull of earth on the stool is greater.

3 Which of the following statements about the moon is NOT correct?

(A) The moon orbits the earth keeping the same side facing us.

(B) The gravitational pull of the moon causes high tides in oceans.

(C) The craters on the moon caused long ago still exist because the moon has no atmosphere.

(D) The sun lights up the complete moon at any one time.

4 A book remains at rest on a table. Why?

(A) No force acts on it.

(B) There is friction between the book and the surface of the table.

(C) Force exerted by the book on the table is the same as the force exerted by the table on the book.

(D) All of the above

5 How is the weight of an astronaut in the the outer space in relation with his actual weight?

(A) It is less than his actual weight.

(B) It is more than his actual weight.

(C) It is the same as his actual weight.

(D) It is zero.

6 Why is the atmospheric pressure not felt by us?

(A) It is small in magnitude.

(B) It acts only on atmosphere and not on us.

(C) Our internal body pressure is equal to that of the atmospheric pressure.

(D) It does not act at sea level.

7 The speed of a falling body increases continuously. Why?

(A) No force acts on the falling body.

(B) The falling body is very light.

(C) Air exerts a frictional force on the falling body.

(D) The force acting on the body is in the direction of the fall.

8 Look at the block placed on the table given below:

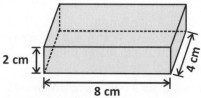

Which of the following physical quantities is not the same when this block is kept over a table with its different faces touching the table?

(A) Pressure   (B) Volume
(C) Weight   (D) Mass

9 Arrange the given pictures in ascending order according to the air pressure at the highest point in each case.

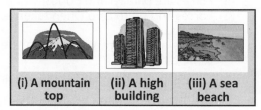

| (i) A mountain top | (ii) A high building | (iii) A sea beach |

(A) (i), (ii), (iii)   (B) (ii), (iii), (i)
(C) (ii), (i), (iii)   (D) (iii), (ii), (i)

10 A spirit level is used to determine the surface level as shown in the figure below.

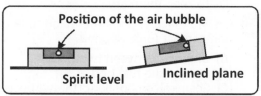

Why does the air bubble at the centre of the tube move to the right when the surface is inclined?

(A) The forces acting on the air bubble are in equilibrium.

(B) Unbalanced forces act on the air bubble.

(C) Air bubbles always rise.

(D) Frictional force act on the air bubble.

Friction

- Friction opposes the relative motion between two surfaces in contact. It acts on both the surfaces.

- Friction depends on the following factors:
  - Material of the bodies in contact.
  - Roughness of the two surfaces in contact. The rougher the surfaces, the greater is the friction.

- The force of friction is independent of the area of the two surfaces in contact.

- The force of friction between two bodies is parallel to the contact surface and always opposite in direction to that of the relative motion.

- Although friction is undesirable, it is important for activities like sitting, walking, braking, etc.

- Friction in machines is reduced by using lubricants and smoothening the surfaces in contact (polishing).

- **Harmful effects of friction:**

  It increases wear and tear
  It produces heat
  It decreases efficiency

- The static friction (or limiting friction) is the friction between any two bodies when one of the bodies just tends to move or slip over the surface of another body. There is no actual movement of the body in static friction.

- Sliding friction (or dynamic friction) comes into play when one of the bodies slides over the other.

- When a body (like a roller or a wheel) rolls over the surface of another body (**e.g.,** road surface), the friction is called rolling friction.

- Rolling friction is much less than sliding friction.

- Liquids and gases (fluids) exert much less friction as compared to solids.

- The frictional force exerted by fluids (including air) is called drag.

- The special shape of a body (object) to reduce drag is called streamlined shape. For **e.g.,** birds and aeroplanes have streamlined shapes.

- Air also exerts friction on a moving body, but it is much smaller as compared to solids and liquids.

Multiple Choice Questions　　A　B　C　D

1 What type of a force is friction?

(A) Contact force
(B) Non-contact force
(C) Electrostatic force
(D) Magnetic force

2 What is the value of sliding friction for an object which requires 7 N of force to move it from rest?

(A) 7 N
(B) Greater than 7 N
(C) Less than 7 N
(D) 14 N

3 Which of the following materials is likely to have the least friction?

(A) Wood　　　　(B) Cardboard
(C) Glass　　　　(D) Paper

4 Which of the following reduces friction in a rotating machine?

(A) Wheels　　　(B) Rollers
(C) Ball bearings　(D) Handle

5 In which of the following cases is friction desirable?

(A) Movement of piston in a cylinder
(B) A vehicle speeding
(C) Running on a track
(D) All of the above

6 Why is a carrom board usually powdered before playing?

(A) For increasing friction
(B) For decreasing friction
(C) For decoration
(D) For fragrance

7 Which of the following statements is *correct*?

(A) Rolling is easier than sliding.
(B) Sliding is easier than rolling.
(C) Dragging is easier than sliding.
(D) Dragging is easier than rolling.

8 What is the frictional force exerted by fluids called?

(A) Lift　　　　　(B) Drag
(C) Rolling friction　(D) Dynamic friction

9 Why are certain bodies streamlined?

(A) To increase friction
(B) To decrease weight
(C) To reduce friction
(D) To increase weight

10 In the decreasing order of magnitude, which of the following is *correct*?

(A) Rolling < static < sliding friction
(B) Static > sliding > rolling friction
(C) Static > rolling > sliding friction
(D) Sliding < static < rolling friction

11 Which of the following activities is easier to perform on a drum of 10 kg?

(A) Dragging the drum
(B) Lifting the drum
(C) Rolling the drum
(D) All of the above need the same effort

12 Why does a meteor burn upon entering the earth's atmosphere?

(A) Due to gravitational pull
(B) Due to the heat of the earth
(C) Due to solar radiation
(D) Due to excess friction in air

13 Why are the head of a match stick and the sides of a match box deliberately made rough?

(A) To increase friction
(B) To decrease friction
(C) To increase the amount of heat
(D) To decrease the amount of heat

14 Why are spikes provided in the shoes of athletes?

(A) As a decoration
(B) To increase friction
(C) To decrease friction
(D) To give shape

15 Which force prevents us from slipping while walking on the road?

(A) Muscular force of our body
(B) Gravitational pull by the earth
(C) Frictional force
(D) Balanced forces of nature

16. Which of the following statements is NOT true?

    (A) Friction can be reduced by converting sliding friction into rolling friction.
    (B) Friction in air and water can be reduced by streamlining the shape of the objects.
    (C) A polished surface will have less friction.
    (D) Friction can be reduced to zero.

17. What will happen to a moving object if there is no friction?

    (A) The object will stop.
    (B) The object will keep on moving.
    (C) The object will change speed.
    (D) The object will change direction.

18. Which of the following is a disadvantage of friction?

    (A) It enables the brakes of a car to work.
    (B) It allows us to hold a pen.
    (C) It helps us to sandpaper a table.
    (D) It wears out our shoes.

19. Which of the following is NOT an effect of frictional force?

    (A) The grooves of tyres flattened due to use
    (B) A rolling ball coming to a halt
    (C) Leaves falling from a tree
    (D) The holding of a pencil

20. Why are tyres made circular in shape?

    (A) It is easy to inflate circular tyres.
    (B) Rolling friction is less than sliding friction.
    (C) Circular tyres dissipate less heat.
    (D) Circular tyres easily slow down or stop a vehicle.

21. Sudhakar's bicycle was making a lot of squeaking noise. What should he do to stop the squeaking noise?

    (A) Water   (B) Oil
    (C) Sand   (D) Powder

22. A coin flicked on a table will stop. Why?

    (A) It is heavy.
    (B) No force is acting on it.
    (C) The earth attracts the coin.
    (D) The table exerts a frictional force.

23. While walking on ice, why should one take small steps to avoid slipping?

    (A) Smaller steps ensure larger friction.
    (B) Smaller steps ensure smaller friction.
    (C) Smaller steps ensure larger distance covered.
    (D) Smaller steps ensure smaller distance covered.

24. In which of the following activities is friction useful?

    (A) Driving a car
    (B) Sitting on a chair
    (C) Rowing a boat
    (D) All of the above

25. How can friction be decreased?

    (A) By using smooth surfaces
    (B) By using dry surfaces
    (C) By increasing the weight of the body
    (D) All of the above

Previous Contest Questions

1. Which of the following is a measure of the force required to keep an object moving with the same speed?

    (A) Static friction
    (B) Sliding friction
    (C) Limiting friction
    (D) All of the above

2. Which of the following activities will not be possible in the absence of friction?

    (A) Holding a glass
    (B) Writing on a paper
    (C) Sitting on a chair
    (D) All of the above

3. Which of the following activities will produce the least amount of frictional force?

    (A) Walking   (B) Running
    (C) Ice-skating   (D) Rowing a boat

4 Which of the following is reduced by the correct measure of air pressure in the tyres?

(A) Static friction (B) Sliding friction
(C) Rolling friction (D) All of the above

5 Which of the following makes it difficult to quickly stop a ship moving in a sea by applying brakes?

(A) Low friction (B) Excess friction
(C) High speed (D) External force

6 When a coin and a feather are dropped simultaneously from the same height, the coin strikes the ground first. Why?

(A) Gravitational force is less in the case of the coin.
(B) Mass of coin is less.
(C) Frictional force is less in the case of the coin.
(D) Magnetic force is stronger in the case of the coin.

7 Why do the soles of our shoes easily wear out?

(A) Due to the difference in the material of the sole
(B) Due to poor design
(C) Due to friction
(D) Due to their size

8 Harish rolled a small steel ball at one edge of the glass bowl as shown below.

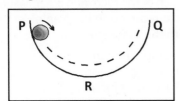

If there is no friction between the surfaces of the ball and the bowl, what will happen to the ball ?

(A) The ball will roll out of the glass bowl near edge 'Q'.
(B) It will stop at centre point 'R' after a number of to-and-fro motions.
(C) It will keep moving between point 'P' and 'Q' and will never stop.
(D) It will not move at all since friction is required for movement.

9 When does a body have zero force of friction ?

(A) When no force is applied on a body at rest
(B) When a large force is applied on a body
(C) When a body is rolling on the surface
(D) When a body is sliding on the surface

10 Look at the figure given below.

Which of the following forces is necessary for a person to climb the mountain?

(A) Gravitational force
(B) Electrical force
(C) Frictional force
(D) Magnetic force

11 Observe the figure given below.

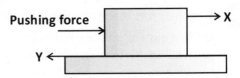

Identify X and Y.

	X	Y
(A)	Motion	Weight
(B)	Motion	Friction
(C)	Friction	Weight
(D)	Weight	Motion

12 Anoop and Sohail while studying about friction decided to perform an experiment. They placed equal masses of an ice block and sand paper block on an inclined plastic tray as shown below.

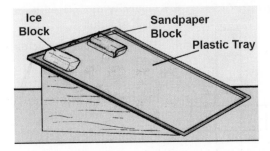

What happens when both the blocks start moving?

(A) Ice block reaches the bottom of the tray first.

(B) Sand paper block reaches the bottom of the tray first.

(C) Both the blocks reach the bottom of the tray at the same time.

(D) Both the blocks offer the same amount of friction.

13 An experiment was conducted to find the amount of force needed to move a 100 g load over different surfaces. Which one of the following scales would show the smallest reading?

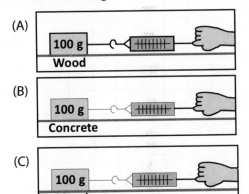

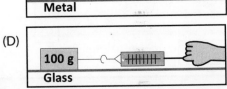

14 In which of the following does friction play a helpful role?

(i)	Striking a match stick
(ii)	Playing snooker
(iii)	Writing on the blackboard

(A) Only (i) and (ii)   (B) Only (ii) and (iii)
(C) Only (i), and (iii) (D) (i), (ii) and (iii)

15 Which of the following shows that friction exists between the two bodies?

(A) When the movement is decreased or prevented

(B) When there is a constant movement

(C) When electromagnetic charges are produced

(D) When there is a constant increase in weight

CROSSWORD

1. Force and Pressure

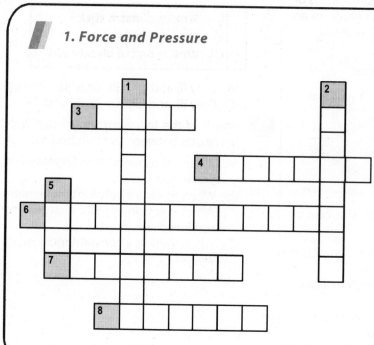

ACROSS

3. Quantity associated with a push or a pull

4. The force applied by actually touching the body

6. The force that attracts massive large objects like the earth, the moon, etc.

7. The force that attracts

8. Type of friction required to keep an object moving

DOWN

1. Force exerted by a surface as an object moves across it

2. The force applied by the arms

5. C.G.S. unit of mass

ACROSS

5. Friction present when a boy plays on the slide

7. The phenomenon caused when a plug is inserted

8. The friction that has the least magnitude in fluids

DOWN

1. Friction present when there is no relative motion between the surfaces in contact

2. Shape necessary to overcome friction

3. Friction that allows a body to be in motion

4. Friction present when a body rolls on the surface

6. Substances that exert less friction than solids

2. Friction

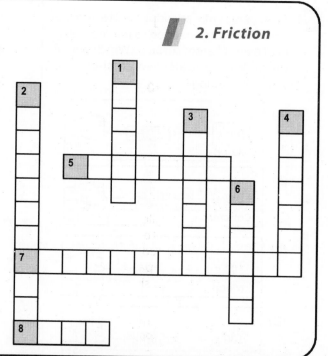

Sound

Synopsis

♦ Sound is a form of energy that produces sensation of hearing in our ears.

♦ Sound is produced when a body vibrates.

♦ Sound needs a medium to travel. It cannot travel in vacuum.

♦ Sound travels faster in solid medium (like wood) as compared to water and air.

♦ All musical instruments have vibrating parts, which produce sound.

♦ In human beings, sound is produced by the voice box or the larynx.

♦ We hear through the vibration of our eardrum, whenever sound reaches our ears.

♦ The number of oscillations per second is called the frequency of oscillation (f) and is expressed in hertz (Hz). A frquency of 1 Hz is one oscillation per second.

♦ The time needed to complete one oscillation is called time period (T). Hence, the number of oscillations per unit time is the frequency of wave $f = 1/T$.

♦ The maximum displacement of the wave crest from the central position on either side is called its amplitude.

♦ We differentiate sounds on the basis of their amplitudes and frequencies.

♦ A human being can hear sound waves within a range of 20 Hz to 20,000 Hz. Some animals like dogs can hear sounds higher than 20,000 Hz.

♦ The larger the amplitude of vibration, the louder is the sound.

♦ Loudness of sound is proportional to the square of the amplitude of the vibration producing the sound. The loudness is expressed in a unit called decibel (dB).

♦ Shrillness or the pitch of a sound depends upon its frequency. Higher the frequency, higher is the pitch and vice-versa.

♦ Unwanted, unpleasant sound is noise. Loud noise produces noise pollution, which is harmful and may cause hearing impairment.

♦ The velocity of sound in air is approx. 330 m s⁻¹ under standard temperature and pressure conditions. It varies with temperature, pressure, humidity and density of medium.

Multiple Choice Questions   (A) (B) (C) (D)

1 When we say that sound travels in a medium, what do we mean?

(A) The particles of the medium travel.
(B) The source travels.
(C) The disturbance travels.
(D) The medium travels.

2 Which of the following correctly represents the speed of sound in solids, liquids and gases in ascending order?

(A) Gas > liquid > solid
(B) Liquid > gas > solid
(C) Liquid > solid > gas
(D) Gas > liquid > gas

3 A person can hear an approaching train when he presses his ear to the railway track faster than one who simply stands on the tracks. What makes this possible?

(A) The vibration of railway tracks
(B) The vibration of air
(C) The speed of sound in solids is more
(D) The hearing ability of the man

4 A person can be identified by his voice. What determines this distinguishing feature?

> (i) Amplitude
> (ii) Pitch
> (iii) Loudness

(A) Only (i)   (B) Only (ii) and (iii)
(C) Only (i) and (iii) (D) (i), (ii) and (iii)

5 In human beings, which of the following produces the sound?

(A) Larynx   (B) Wind pipe
(C) Eardrum   (D) Lungs

6 An object oscillates 50 times in one second. What is its frequency?

(A) 0.2 Hz   (B) 0.02 Hz
(C) 0.002 Hz   (D) 50 Hz

7 In which of the three media does sound travel the fastest?

(A) Air
(B) Water
(C) Steel
(D) Speed is same in any medium

8 Flash and thunder are produced simultaneously. But thunder is heard a few seconds after the flash is seen. Why?

(A) The speed of sound is greater than the speed of light.
(B) The speed of sound is equal to the speed of light.
(C) The speed of light is greater than the speed of sound.
(D) All of the above

9 What is the cause for the difference in the voices of men, women and children?

(A) Difference in larynx
(B) Difference in lungs
(C) Difference in vocal cords
(D) Difference in wind pipe

10 Which of the following represents Hertz?

(A) Second   (B) Second^{-1}
(C) Metre   (D) Metre^{-1}

11 On what factors does the loudness or intensity of sound depend?

(A) The amplitude of a sound wave
(B) The area of a vibrating body
(C) Distance from the source of sound
(D) All of the above

12 On what factors does the pitch of sound depend?

(A) Frequency
(B) Amplitude
(C) Loudness
(D) The distance from source

13 Which of the following produces sound in birds?

(A) Vocal cords   (B) Larynx
(C) Glottis   (D) Syrinx

14 Find the difference between a musical sound and noise.

(A) Amplitude   (B) Loudness
(C) Vibrations   (D) All of the above

15 Which of the following are the effects of noise pollution?

(i) **Insomnia**
(ii) **Hypertension**
(iii) **Hearing impairment**

(A) Only (i) and (ii)   (B) Only (ii) and (iii)
(C) Only (i) and (iii)   (D) (i), (ii) and (iii)

16 Which of the following frequencies cannot be heard by human beings?

(A) 1000 Hz   (B) 10,000 Hz
(C) 100 Hz   (D) 1,00,000 Hz

17 Identify the three delicate bones in the middle ear.

(A) Pinna, anvil and cochlea
(B) Hammer, anvil and cochlea
(C) Pinna, eardrum and anvil
(D) Hammer, anvil and stirrup

18 Identify the nerve that carries the signals from the ear to the brain.

(A) The auditory nerve
(B) The optic nerve
(C) The motor nerve
(D) The spinal cord

19 Which of the following helps human beings in producing sounds?

(A) The eardrum
(B) The auditory nerve
(C) The optical cortex
(D) The vocal cords

20 What is the number of vibrations made by a body in one second called?

(A) Frequency   (B) Wavelength
(C) Loudness   (D) Pitch

21 Which instrument always produces vibrations of the same frequency?

(A) A speaker   (B) A bell jar
(C) An electric bell   (D) A tuning fork

22 How is a musical note characterised by?

(A) Loudness
(B) Pitch
(C) Timbre
(D) All of the above

23 On what factors does the frequency of sound depend in wind instruments?

(A) The length of the air column
(B) The breadth of the air column
(C) The force with which the wind is blown
(D) All of the above

24 What happens to the pitch, when we tighten the strings of a guitar?

(A) It increases
(B) It decreases
(C) It remains the same
(D) It may increase or decrease

25 Which of the following *correctly* describes the pitch and the frequency of the sound of a girl's scream?

(A) Low pitch, low frequency
(B) Low pitch, high frequency
(C) High pitch, low frequency
(D) High pitch, high frequency

Previous Contest Questions

1 When a tuning fork was struck and brought near a bucket of water, a wave as shown in the figure, was formed on its surface.

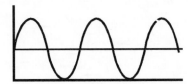

If the fork is struck harder and brought near the surface, what will increase?

(A) Frequency   (B) Wavelength
(C) Velocity   (D) Amplitude

2 How does a whistle produce sound?

(A) The body of whistle stores air.
(B) The air vibrates.
(C) The person produces vibrations.
(D) All of the above

3 Why are sounds of different frequencies produced when the length of the scale protruding out of table is changed and then vibrated ?

(A) Due to change in length
(B) Due to change in velocity
(C) Due to change in amplitude
(D) All of the above

4 If you go on increasing the stretching force on a wire in a guitar, what happens to its frequency?

(A) It increases
(B) It decreases
(C) It remains unchanged
(D) It cannot be said

5 A bomb explodes on the moon. How long will it take for the sound to reach the earth?

(A) 10 seconds
(B) 1000 seconds
(C) 1 day
(D) Sound will not be heard

6 Which is true of a body that vibrates with a higher frequency of 2,00,000 Hz?

(A) It does not always produce sound.
(B) Shrill sounds are produced, which human being can hear.
(C) Dolphins can hear the sound.
(D) All of the above

7 Which of the following is expressed in decibels?

(A) Loudness and amplitude of sound
(B) Loudness and pitch of sound
(C) Amplitude and pitch of sound
(D) Frequency of sound

8 How can the brain interpret the frequency of a sound?

(A) By the loudness of sound
(B) By the frequency of sound
(C) By the pitch of sound
(D) By the amplitude of sound

9 In a stethoscope, how does the sound of heart beat travel through its tube?

(A) By bending along the tube
(B) In a straight line
(C) By undergoing multiple reflections
(D) As ultrasonic frequency

10 The frequency of a source is 15 kHz. What will be the frequency of the sound wave produced by it in water and air?

(A) It is the same as that of the source.
(B) Frequency in water will be more than that in air.
(C) Frequency in air will be more than that in water.
(D) Depends upon the velocities of sound in these media.

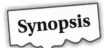

Synopsis

◆ Materials which allow electric current to pass through them are good conductors of electricity. **e.g.,** Metals.

◆ Materials which do not allow electric current to pass through them are bad conductors of electricity. **e.g.,** Wood, Plastic, etc.

◆ Human body is a good conductor of electricity. Thus, we should take precautions while handling electrical appliances.

◆ A bulb glows due to the passage of electric current since the filament of the bulb is heated to a very high temperature. However, if the current through a circuit is too weak, the filament does not get heated sufficiently and it does not glow.

◆ An LED (Light Emitting Diode) glows even when a weak (small) electric current flows through it.

◆ Electric current produces a magnetic effect. It causes a compass needle to deflect.

◆ Pure water (distilled water) is a poor conductor of electricity.

◆ Most liquids that conduct electricity are solutions of acids, bases and salts.

◆ The passage of an electric current through a conducting solution causes chemical reactions. As a result any of the following activities can be observed.
   (a) Formation of gas bubbles.
   (b) Deposit of metals on electrodes.
   (c) Change in colour of the solution.

◆ When electricity is passed through some substances, they decompose. Such reactions are called electrolytic reactions. This chemical effect is used to extract elements in metallurgy and for electroplating.

◆ The process of depositing a layer of any desired metal on another metal by passing electricity is called electroplating.

◆ Chromium plating is done to make the object scratch proof and shiny.

◆ Tin cans used to preserve food items/soft drinks are made by electroplating tin onto iron.

◆ A coating of zinc is deposited on iron to protect it from corrosion and rust.

◆ CFL's (Compact Flourescent Light) consumes less electricity as compared to electric bulb and LED's, but contains mercury which is toxic and poses a disposal problem.

Multiple Choice Questions

1 What is current?

(A) The flow of matter
(B) The flow of electrons
(C) The flow of protons
(D) The flow of charge

2 In electrolytic solutions, which of the following acts as carrier of charge?

(A) Protons   (B) Electrons
(C) Neutrons   (D) Ions

3 What are insulators?

(A) Materials that conduct electricity
(B) Materials that do not conduct electricity
(C) Materials that conduct electricity only at low temperatures
(D) Materials that conduct electricity at room temperature

4 Which of the following is an insulator?

(A) Wood   (B) Iron
(C) Graphite   (D) Silver

5 Which of the following circuits gives the correct way of connecting an LED to light it up?

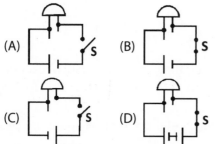

6 Which of the following energy conversions takes place in a cell?

(A) Electrical energy into chemical energy
(B) Chemical energy into electrical energy
(C) Magnetic energy into electrical energy
(D) Electrical energy into mechanical energy

7 Which of the following are the characteristics of an electrolyte?

(A) It has a positive charge.
(B) It has a negative charge.
(C) It conducts charge without dissociating.
(D) It forms positive and negative ions.

8 Which acid is present in lemon juice that acts as an electrolyte?

(A) Sulphuric acid
(B) Nitric acid
(C) Hydrochloric acid
(D) Citric acid

9 Which of the following is the electrolyte in a dry cell?

(A) Copper sulphate
(B) Zinc sulphate
(C) Sulphuric acid
(D) Ammonium chloride

10 In a dry cell, which of the following acts as the positive terminal?

(A) Carbon rod
(B) Manganese dioxide
(C) Manganese dioxide and powdered carbon
(D) A metal cap on the carbon rod

11 What is the common voltage produced by a dry cell ?

(A) 1.5 V   (B) 30 V
(C) 60 V   (D) 3 V

12 What happens when electric current is made to flow through a conductor?

(A) Some amount of electrical energy is converted into heat energy.
(B) Some amount of electrical energy is converted into mechanical energy.
(C) Some amount of mechanical energy is converted into electrical energy.
(D) Some amount of heat energy is converted into electrical energy.

13. Nichrome is an alloy. Which of the following metals make up this alloy?

(A) Nickel and chromium
(B) Nitrogen and chromium
(C) Nitrogen, chlorine and chromium
(D) Nickel, chromium and manganese

14. What is the splitting of a compound using electricity called?

(A) Electrolysis
(B) Electrolyte
(C) Electrokinesis
(D) Electrochemistry

15. What is the principle involved in the glowing of an electric bulb?

(A) Magnetic effect of current
(B) Heating effect of current
(C) Chemical effect
(D) Conduction of current

16. Why are LED's extensively used to replace bulbs?

(i) Consume less electricity
(ii) Have longer life
(iii) Have more power

(A) Only (i) and (ii)   (B) Only (ii) and (iii)
(C) Only (i) and (iii) (D) (i), (ii) and (iii)

17. Which of the following is the best conductor of electricity?

(A) Tap water   (B) Distilled water
(C) Sea water   (D) Rain water

18. Which of the following effects of current is responsible for the deflection of a compass needle in an electric field?

(A) Heating effect of current
(B) Magnetic effect of current
(C) Conducting effect of heat
(D) Chemical effect of current

19. Which of these is the industrial applications of the chemical effects of electric current?

(A) Electroplating
(B) Galvanising
(C) Anodising
(D) All of the above

20. Which of the following liquids is a bad conductor of electricity?

(A) Lemon juice
(B) Vinegar
(C) Sea water
(D) Distilled water

21. Cans used for storing food are electroplated. What is the material used for electroplating?

(A) Chrome onto tin
(B) Iron onto tin
(C) Tin onto iron
(D) Chrome onto iron

22. What is iron coated with in order to protect it from corrosion and rust ?

(A) Tin   (B) Copper
(C) Zinc   (D) Mercury

23. Why is zinc better than tin for electroplating a piece of iron in order to prevent it from rusting ?

(A) Zinc is cheaper than tin.
(B) Tin is toxic.
(C) Zinc can prevent iron from coming into contact with water and air.
(D) Rusting is prevented even when the zinc layer is broken.

24. Which of the following statements is *correct*?

(A) Distilled water is a good conductor of electricity.
(B) An LED glows even when a weak electric current flows through it.
(C) Only hydrated salt solutions conduct electricity.
(D) Zinc plating is done to make the object scratch proof.

25. 'X' is a good conductor of electricity. Which of the following could be 'X'?

(A) Solid sodium chloride
(B) Vinegar
(C) Distilled water
(D) Liquid oxygen

Previous Contest Questions

1 In a cell, by convention, from where does the charge seem to be flowing through?

(A) From positive electrode to negative electrode
(B) From negative electrode to positive electrode
(C) Both (A) and (B)
(D) Cannot be said

2 Why are metals good conductors of electricity?

(A) In metals, outer electrons are strongly bound to the atom.
(B) In metals, outer electrons are loosely bound to the atom.
(C) In metals, inner electrons are loosely bound to the atom.
(D) In metals, protons can detach from the nucleus and conduct electricity.

3 Why are cans used for storing soft drinks or food items usually electroplated with tin?

(A) Tin is less reactive than the metal the can is made of.
(B) Tin is cheap.
(C) Tin is strong and shiny in appearance
(D) Tin is lighter than other metals.

4 During the electrolysis of $CuSO_4$ solution, sulphate ions move towards the

(A) copper electrode.
(B) anode.
(C) cathode.
(D) zinc electrode.

5 A bulb does not glow when the probes are hanging in air. Why?

(A) Air absorbs electricity.
(B) Air is a bad conductor of electricity.
(C) Electricity is discharged into air.
(D) Air disperses electricity.

6 Iron vessels are coated with tin to

(A) give better shining.
(B) increase the strength.
(C) increase weight.
(D) prevent rusting.

7 Observe the given figure.

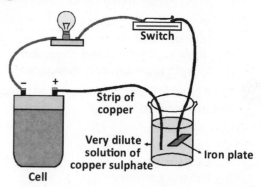

What is the purpose of this experimental setup?

(A) To check the conductivity of copper sulphate solution.
(B) To get iron electroplated.
(C) To check the continuity of charge flow in the circuit.
(D) To make the electric bulb glow.

8 What is the process of depositing a layer of a desired metal on another material by passing electric current called?

(A) Electrolysis
(B) Electroplating
(C) Chromium plating
(D) Galvanising

9 Which of the following statements is NOT correct?

(A) The ions are free to move about in an electrolyte.
(B) The solution which can form ions is used for electroplating.
(C) Acids are bad conductors of electricity.
(D) An electric bulb glows due to the heating effect of current.

10 The charges present on the various objects are shown below in the figure. In which of the following cases does a force of repulsion act between them?

(A) (+3 C)　(+3 C)　(B) (−3 C)　(+3 C)

(C) (+3 C)　(0 C)　(D) (−3 C)　(0 C)

CROSSWORD

3. Sound

ACROSS

2. That through which sound does not propagate.
6. The characteristic feature of sound waves
8. The periodic vibration of sound
10. The characteristic of sound that distinguishes between loud and feeble sound
11. Reflection of sound
12. Non-periodic vibration of sound
13. The characteristic of sound that depends on the frequency of sound

DOWN

1. High pitch sound
3. Maximum displacement of a vibrating body
4. Number of vibrations produced in one second
5. Frequency of sound below 20 Hz
7. Distance between two consecutive compressions
9. Finding the depth of the sea

ACROSS

1. The process of depositing a layer of a desired metal on another metal by passing electricity
7. The positive terminal
8. Positive ions
9. The negative terminal
10. The process of the decomposition of substances when electricity is passed through them

DOWN

2. The metal used for electroplating to make the object scratch proof and appear shiny
3. Liquids which dissociate into ions when electric current passes through them
4. Metal plates which are partly immersed in the electrolyte to pass current through them
5. Liquids which do not allow passage of electric current through them
6. Negative ions

4. Chemical Effects of Electric Current

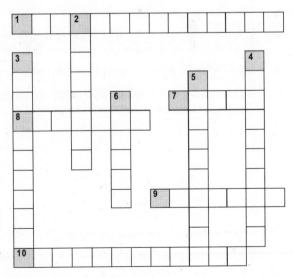

Some Natural Phenomena

Synopsis

◆ High speed winds are accompanied by reduced air pressure.

◆ Air moves from a region of high pressure to low pressure.

◆ A thunderstorm occurs due to strong, upward rising winds along with swift movement of the falling water droplets carried with lightning and sound.

◆ A thunderstorm may develop into a cyclone or a hurricane with wind speed being as high as 200 km h^{-1}.

◆ A tornado is a dark, funnel shaped cloud that reaches the ground from the sky. A tornado may form within cyclones and can reach a speed upto 300 km h^{-1}.

◆ Electroscope is an instrument used to detect the presence of electric charge on a body.

◆ An electrical charge can be transferred from a charged object to another through a metal conductor.

◆ The process of transferring charge from a charged body to the earth is called earthing.

◆ Lightning takes place when large amount of accumulated charges in the clouds passes onto the earth through atmosphere.

◆ Lightning conductors are used to protect tall buildings from the effect of lightning.

◆ An earthquake takes place due to disturbance inside the earth's crust.

◆ The weak zones on the earth's crust, prone to earthquakes, are known as seismic or fault zones.

◆ The power of an earthquake is expressed in terms of its magnitude on a scale called the Richter scale. Higher the magnitude, greater is the damage.

◆ Seismographs are instruments which record tremors produced by the earth.

◆ Lightning, cyclones and earthquakes can cause extensive damage to mankind and properties. We should take necessary steps to protect ourselves during such natural calamities.

Multiple Choice Questions   Ⓐ Ⓑ Ⓒ Ⓓ

1 What is the force present between two charged bodies called?

(A) Electrostatic force
(B) Electromagnetic force
(C) Gravitational force
(D) Frictional force

2 What happens when two bodies are rubbed against each other ?

(A) They acquire equal and similar charges.
(B) They acquire equal and opposite charges.
(C) They acquire different charges but in different amounts depending upon their masses.
(D) They do not acquire any charge.

3 Suppose you are in a car and there is a thunderstorm. Which of the following is the best way to protect yourself from possible harm?

(A) Remaining in the car
(B) Getting out of the car and taking cover under the car
(C) Running to a nearby tree
(D) Getting out and standing under an electric pole

4 What is the S.I. unit of electric charge?

(A) Coulomb   (B) Ampere
(C) Volt   (D) Watt

5 What happens when an ebonite rod rubbed with fur and a glass rod rubbed with silk are brought near each other?

(A) They attract each other.
(B) They repel each other.
(C) Nothing happens to them.
(D) They acquire heat.

6 What are lightning rods made up of?

(A) Copper   (B) Plastic
(C) Bakelite   (D) Sand paper

7 What is the purpose of an electroscope ?

(A) To detect and test small electric charges
(B) To calculate the amount of electric charge flowing through the conductor
(C) To find out the presence of antimatter
(D) To test the presence of magnetic field

8 Why is a lightning conductor installed on a building?

(A) So that it collects the electric power present in the lightning
(B) So that it repels the lightning that falls on the building
(C) So that it forces the lightning to fall in an area where there are no buildings
(D) So that it conducts electric charge to the ground when lightning strikes the building

9 What happens when a glass rod is rubbed with silk cloth?

(A) Electrons are added to it.
(B) Electrons are removed from it.
(C) Protons are added to it.
(D) Protons are removed from it.

10 When you touch a charged body, the charge flows through you into the earth. What is this called?

(A) Induction   (B) Conduction
(C) Capacitance   (D) Earthing

11 What is the nature of electrical charges generated by rubbing two objects?

(A) Static   (B) Mobile
(C) Positive   (D) Negative

12 Which layer of the earth is exposed to the atmosphere?

(A) Outer core   (B) Mantle
(C) Inner core   (D) Crust

13 Which fundamental particle in an atom has no charge?

(A) Electron   (B) Proton
(C) Neutron   (D) Both (A) and (B)

14 When we remove polyester or woollen clothes in dark, we can see a spark and hear a crackling sound. Which of the following is responsible for it?

(A) Static electricity
(B) Current electricity
(C) Positive charge
(D) Negative charge

15 Which of the following allows the transfer of electric charge from one charged object to another?

(A) Vacuum   (B) Air
(C) Insulator   (D) Conductor

16 What is the lightning streaks that we see?

(A) UV rays from the sun
(B) Cosmic rays
(C) Accumulated electric charges
(D) IR rays from the sun

17 Which of the following is the safest way to protect yourself from lightning?

(A) Run into an open field
(B) Open an umbrella for cover
(C) Take shelter under a tree
(D) Squat low on the ground

18 Which of the following countries in the world is most prone to earthquakes?
(A) India   (B) America
(C) China   (D) Japan

19 What are high speed winds accompanied with?

(A) Increased pressure
(B) Reduced pressure
(C) Water vapour
(D) Static electricity

20 By which of the following methods can a body be charged?

(A) Conduction   (B) Induction
(C) Friction   (D) All of the above

21 Which natural calamity cannot be predicted accurately in advance?

(A) Flood   (B) Cyclone
(C) Earthquake   (D) Famine

22 What are the weak zones that are present around the boundaries of plates underneath the earth and cause slides and earthquakes commonly known as?

(A) Fault zones   (B) Eruption zones
(C) Explosive zones (D) Sliding zones

23 On which of the following scales is the magnitude of an earthquake measured?

(A) Celsius   (B) Richter
(C) Fahrenheit   (D) Both (A) and (B)

24 In which of the following states is an earthquake most likely to occur?

(A) Gujarat   (B) Chhatisgarh
(C) Chennai   (D) Kerala

25 Which of the following is caused by electric sparks?

(A) Thunder   (B) Lightning
(C) Storm   (D) Cyclone

Previous Contest Questions

1 According to the law of electrostatics,

(A) a charged body attracts similar charged bodies but repels uncharged bodies.
(B) a charged body attracts bodies carrying similar charge and repels bodies possessing opposite charge.
(C) a charged body repels bodies possessing similar charge and attracts bodies with opposite charge.
(D) a charged body attracts all types of charged bodies.

2 Which of the following is/are affected during lightning?

(A) T.V.   (B) Radio
(C) Telephone   (D) All of the above

3. How is lightning useful to us?

(A) It helps in nitrogen fixation and promotes plant growth.
(B) Ozone is formed which prevents ultraviolet rays falling on the earth.
(C) It helps in the evolution of a new species.
(D) All of the above

4. What happens when water vapour changes to liquid in the form of rain drops?

(A) Heat is absorbed.
(B) Heat is released.
(C) Heat is first absorbed and then released.
(D) There is no release of heat.

5. Which of the following statements is NOT true?

(A) Lightning and sparks from woollen clothing are essentially the same phenomena.
(B) When you rub a plastic scale on dry hair, it acquires charge.
(C) A glass rod when rubbed with silk acquires negative charge.
(D) Static charges are called so, because they do not move by themselves.

6. Which of the following makes the outermost layer of the earth fragmented?

(A) Crust   (B) Plate
(C) Core   (D) Inner zone

7. Earthquakes at two places M and N were measured as 2 and 4. How is the magnitude and their destructive energy at M and N related?

(A) Tremor at N is strong as that at place 'M'.
(B) Tremor at N is four times stronger than that at place 'M'.
(C) Tremor at N is 100 times stronger than that at place 'M'.
(D) Tremor at N is 1000 times stronger than that at place 'M'.

8. Where is the crust of the earth the thickest?

(A) At the continents
(B) At the ocean
(C) At the poles
(D) Near faults

9. Which of the following events can cause an earthquake?

(i) **Movement of earth's plates**
(ii) **Volcanic eruption**
(iii) **Underground nuclear explosion**

(A) Only (i) and (ii)   (B) Only (ii) and (iii)
(C) Only (i) and (iii)   (D) (i), (ii) and (iii)

10. On what factors does the response of the rock to stress depend ?

(i) **Its temperature**
(ii) **The speed of stress applied**
(iii) **The confining pressure on the rock**

(A) Only (i) and (ii)   (B) Only (ii) and (iii)
(C) Only (i) and (iii)   (D) (i), (ii) and (iii)

CHAPTER 6

Light

Synopsis

◆ Light is a form of energy. It is an electromagnetic radiation which can travel through vacuum with a speed of 3×10^8 m s^{-1}. Light travels along straight lines. This property is known as the rectilinear propagation of light. We can see an object only when it reflects or scatters the light falling on it.

◆ Any polished or shining surface acts as a mirror and regular reflection takes place.

◆ When there is no regular reflection, sharp images are not obtained and so they cannot be seen by us. This happens because of scattering of light due to irregular reflection.

◆ An image which can be obtained on a screen is called a real image.

◆ An image which cannot be obtained on a screen is called a virtual image.

◆ The image formed by a plane mirror is erect. It is virtual and is of the same size as the object. The image is at the same distance behind the mirror as the object is in front of it. In an image formed by a plane mirror, the left side of the object is seen on the right side in the image, and right side of the object appears to be on the left side in the image. This is known as lateral inversion.

◆ If two plane mirrors are placed at an angle between them, a number of images are formed. If the angle between the mirrors is θ, then the number of images formed "n" is given by the formula,

$$n = \left[\frac{360}{\theta} - 1\right], \text{if } \frac{360}{\theta} \text{ is even and } n = \frac{360}{\theta}, \text{if it is odd.}$$

◆ White light is composed of seven colours.

◆ The splitting of light into seven colours is known as dispersion of light. Rainbow is a natural phenomenon showing dispersion.

◆ Human eye consists of structures like cornea, iris and pupil.

◆ Visually challenged persons (blind) can read and write using the Braille code.

Multiple Choice Questions   Ⓐ Ⓑ Ⓒ Ⓓ

1 'X' is a surface that cannot produce clear images. What is 'X'?

(A) Rough surface
(B) Ideal surface
(C) Smooth surface
(D) Smooth but curved surface

2 With what is glass coated in order to convert it into a mirror?

(A) Silver   (B) Copper
(C) Aluminium   (D) Platinum

3 What makes objects visible?

(A) The absorption of light by objects
(B) The reflected light from the object
(C) The total internal reflection taking place in an object
(D) The refracted light from the object

4 What is the phenomenon of light bouncing back into the same medium called?

(A) Reflection   (B) Refraction
(C) Dispersion   (D) Splitting

5 What is the perpendicular drawn at any point on a mirror called?

(A) Incident ray   (B) Reflected ray
(C) Normal   (D) Image

6 How many images are obtained when plane mirrors are arranged parallel to each other?

(A) A single image
(B) Two images
(C) Infinite number of images
(D) Zero image

7 If the angle of incidence is 80°, what will be the angle of reflection?

(A) 80°   (B) 100°
(C) 160°   (D) 20°

8 Which of the following is used by E.N.T. doctors?

(A) Convex mirror (B) Convex lens
(C) Plane mirror   (D) Concave mirror

9 When the angle between two plane mirrors is 60°, how many images will be formed by the mirrors?

(A) 5   (B) 6
(C) 7   (D) 8

10 If the angle of incidence is 50°, then calculate the angle between the incident ray and the reflected ray.

(A) 50°   (B) 100°
(C) 130°   (D) 80°

11 In our houses, which of the following is used for looking at ourselves?

(A) Convex mirror
(B) Concave mirror
(C) Convex lens
(D) Plane mirror

12 Which of the following statements is *true*?

(A) The angle of incidence is twice the angle of reflection.
(B) The incident ray, the reflected ray and the normal drawn at the point of incidence lie in the same plane.
(C) Some virtual images can be caught on the screen.
(D) A convex mirror forms a real image.

13 What happens in lateral inversion?

(A) The right side of the object will be on the right side of the image.
(B) The left side of the object will be on the left side of the image.
(C) The top of the object will be the bottom of the object.
(D) The right side of the object will be on the left side of the image.

14 In a periscope, how are the reflecting mirrors arranged?

(A) Perpendicular to each other
(B) Parallel to each other
(C) At an angle of 90⁰
(D) At an angle of 60⁰

15 What is the nature of image formed on the retina of human eye of an object ?

(A) Virtual and erect
(B) Virtual and inverted
(C) Real and erect
(D) Real and inverted

16 Identify the value of persistence of vision.

(A) 1/10th of a second
(B) 1/12th of a second
(C) 1/16th of a second
(D) 1/20th of a second

17 The characteristics of an eye disease are given below.

> **(i) Eye sight becomes foggy**
> **(ii) Eye lens becomes cloudy**
> **(iii) There is a loss of vision**

In which of the following are the above characteristics observed?

(A) Myopia   (B) Presbyopia
(C) Hypermetropia   (D) Cataract

18 Which of the following is the requirement of nocturnal animals like owl and bat?

(A) Large cornea
(B) Large pupil
(C) Retina with large number of rods
(D) All of the above

19 Look at the given figure.

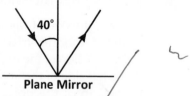

Plane Mirror

Find the angle between the incident ray and the reflected ray.

(A) 60°   (B) 90°   (C) 80°   (D) 40°

20 The diagram shows the path of a light ray X, directed at a plane mirror.

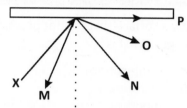

Which of the following is the correct reflected ray?

(A) M   (B) N
(C) O   (D) P

21 For a given incident ray, the plane of the mirror makes an angle θ with the incident ray, then the reflected ray is turned through 2θ. Which of the following is based on the above principle?

(A) Periscope
(B) Kaleidoscope
(C) Shaving mirrors
(D) Automobile head lights

22 An object placed 4 m from a plane mirror is shifted by 0.5 m away from the mirror. What is the distance between the object and its image?

(A) 4 m   (B) 3.5 m
(C) 9 m   (D) 5 m

23 There are 11 letters in the word EXAMINATION. How many letters of this word are not changed when the word is seen in a plane mirror?

(A) 11   (B) 5   (C) 8   (D) 9

24 Observe the figure given below.

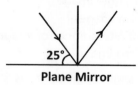

Plane Mirror

Find the angle between the incident ray and the reflected ray.

(A) 65°   (B) 90°   (C) 130°   (D) 25°

25 How is a rainbow formed?

(A) When raindrops absorb sunlight
(B) When raindrops reflect sunlight
(C) When raindrops disperse sunlight
(D) When raindrops diffract sunlight

Previous Contest Questions

1 Which of the following letters will be seen without any change in a plane mirror?

(A) S   (B) T
(C) L   (D) P

2 Which of the following is the characteristic of an ideal mirror?

(A) It absorbs all the amount of light incident on it.
(B) It refracts all the light.
(C) It reflects all the light.
(D) All of the above

3 In which of the following are plane mirrors arranged at an angle to get a number of coloured images?

(A) Periscope   (B) Kaleidoscope
(C) Telescope   (D) Thermoscope

4 A series of fast moving still pictures can create an illusion of movement. Why?

(A) The eye can focus on very rapidly changing pictures.
(B) The eye is quicker than the brain.
(C) The eye can separate two images only when the interval of separation between them is one-sixteenth of a second.
(D) The optical cortex can see through the rapidly moving images.

5 Which of the following prevents internal reflections of light inside the human eye?

(A) Iris   (B) Pupil
(C) Choroid   (D) Blind spot

6 For a normal eye, in an adult, what is the least distance of distinct vision?

(A) 5 to 8 cm   (B) 10 to 15 cm
(C) 20 to 25 cm   (D) 30 to 35 cm

7 Identify the part of the human eye on which different images are formed.

(A) Iris   (B) Pupil
(C) Cornea   (D) Retina

8 Identify the nature of the image formed by the eye lens of a human eye.

(A) Real, upright and enlarged
(B) Real, upright and diminished
(C) Real, inverted and diminished
(D) Virtual, inverted and diminished

9 Which of the following occurs in persons suffering from myopia?

(A) The eye ball is shortened.
(B) Ciliary muscles contract.
(C) The eye ball elongates.
(D) The retina expands.

10 According to the laws of reflection, which of the following statements is *correct*?

(A) The angle of incidence is greater than the angle of reflection.
(B) The angle of incidence is less than the angle of reflection.
(C) The angle of incidence is equal to the angle of reflection.
(D) The angle of incidence is not equal to the angle of reflection.

CROSSWORD

5. Some Natural Phenomena

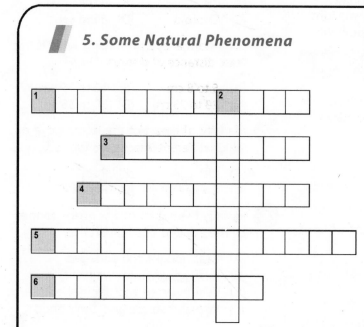

ACROSS

1. A device used for detecting the presence of an electric charge

3. One that is caused by the accumulation of charges in the clouds

4. The sudden shaking of the earth lasting for a short time

5. The study of static electrical charges

6. Substances which do not have free electrons

DOWN

2. Substances which have free electrons

ACROSS

1. Part of the eye that refracts light and focusses the image on the retina

3. The perpendicular drawn to the surface at the point of incidence

4. Light rays that meet at a point.

7. A real image is always

8. One that allows light to enter the eye ball

9. Substances that allow most of the light to pass through them

10. Irregular reflection is

11. Focusses light and forms an image of the object on the retina

12. Device used in submarines to see objects above water surface

DOWN

1. One that absorbs light and prevents reflection in the eyeball

2. Phenomenon in which a bulb is made to glow with heat

5. A body that emits light on its own

6. Image formed by a divergent reflected beam

6. Light

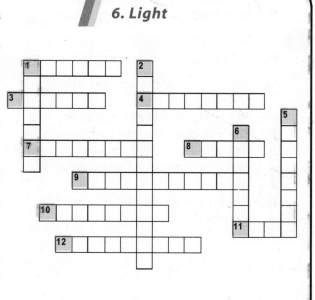

CHAPTER 7

Stars and The Solar System

Synopsis

- Universe is a vast collection of stars, planets, nebulae, galaxies, intergalactic matter and everything that exists in them. It is believed to have been formed 15 billion years ago from a huge explosion called 'Big Bang'.

- To measure distances on astronomical scale, the unit 'light year' is used. It is the distance travelled by light in one year. 1 light year = 9.46×10^{12} km.

- Stars are self-luminous, astronomical bodies which produce energy from nuclear fusion reactions. They form from a large collection of gases called nebulae.

- A galaxy is a group of billion stars and other celestial bodies. Galaxies exist in different shapes such as circular, elliptical, ring and irregular. They usually revolve around themselves and move away from each other at tremendous speeds.

- A group of stars which seem to form a pattern is called a constellation.
  e.g., Big bear, Orion etc.

- Sun along with its nine planets, their satellites, asteroids and comets are together named as solar system.

- Planets like Mercury, Venus and Mars have internal structures similar to that of the earth. So, they are called terrestrial planets. Jupiter, Uranus, Saturn and Neptune are mainly made up of gases. They are called gas planets.

- Asteroids are irregular, rocky bodies that revolve around the sun between the orbits of Mars and Jupiter.

- A comet is a small body of rocks, ice and gases that revolve around the sun in a highly eccentric, elliptical orbit.

- A man-made spacecraft orbiting around an astronomical body is called a satellite. If the orbit of a satellite is synchronised with the earth's rotation, it is called a geostationary satellite. If a satellite seems to be stationary from the point of view of the sun, it is called the sun synchronous or polar satellite.

- Satellites are used for communication, weather forecasts, remote sensing, conducting scientific experiments and for various other military uses.

- The various shapes of the bright part of the moon as seen during a month are called phases of moon.

- A planet has a definite path in which it revolves around the sun. This path is called an orbit.

- The axis of earth is inclined to its orbital plane at an angle of 66.5°. This inclination helps in the change of seasons on the earth.

- The time taken by a planet to complete one revolution around the sun is called the period of revolution, while the time taken to complete one round around its own axis is called the period of rotation.

Multiple Choice Questions   (A) (B) (C) (D)

1 Which of the following physical quantities has light year as its unit ?

(A) Time　　　　(B) Intensity of light
(C) Illumination　(D) Distance

2 Identify the closest star to our solar system.

(A) Proxima centauri
(B) Sirius
(C) Swati
(D) Ashwini

3 What are groups of stars which seem to form a pattern called ?

(A) Nebulae　　　(B) Galaxies
(C) Asteroids　　 (D) Constellations

4 What is the approximate height of a geostationary satellite?

(A) 6,400 km　　　(B) 12,800 km
(C) 7,200 km　　　(D) 36,000 km

5 Which of the following is the first Indian satellite?

(A) INSAT　　　　(B) Aryabhatta
(C) Bhaskara　　 (D) APPLE

6 What kind of a planet is Jupiter?

(A) Terrestrial planet
(B) Gas planet
(C) Asteroid
(D) Hottest planet

7 How do stars appear to move?

(A) From east to west
(B) From west to east
(C) From north to south
(D) From south to north

8 To which of the following category does Orion belong?

(A) Star　　　　　(B) Planet
(C) Galaxy　　　　(D) Constellation

9 Which planet has "the great red spot"?

(A) Mars　　　　　(B) Venus
(C) Jupiter　　　　(D) Mercury

10 Where is a spy satellite deployed?

(A) Low-earth orbit
(B) Geostationary orbit
(C) Polar orbit
(D) Both (A) and (B)

11 What is Ceres?

(A) A satellite of Mars
(B) A satellite of Jupiter
(C) An asteroid
(D) A meteorite that fell over Siberia in 1908

12 Which of the following is the brightest non-star visible to the human eye?

(A) Moon　　　　　(B) Venus
(C) Mars　　　　　(D) Jupiter

13 Which is the only moon in the solar system with active volcanoes?

(A) Moon　　　　　(B) Io
(C) Titan　　　　　(D) Ganymede

14 Which is the largest, natural satellite in the solar system?

(A) The moon　　　(B) Io
(C) Eros　　　　　(D) Ganymede

15 Which of the following planets can be seen with naked eyes?

(A) Mercury, Venus, Uranus, Jupiter
(B) Mars, Jupiter, Uranus, Neptune
(C) Mercury, Venus, Uranus, Pluto
(D) Mercury, Mars, Venus, Jupiter

16 In which orbits do satellites revolve?

(A) Circular and hyperbolic orbits
(B) Elliptical and parabolic orbits
(C) Elliptical and circular orbits
(D) Only in elliptical orbits

17 Identify the biggest constellation.

(A) Sirius　　　　 (B) Hydra
(C) Andromeda　　(D) Ursa minor

18 Of which element is ozone made?

(A) Oxygen
(B) Nitrogen
(C) Carbon
(D) Carbon and oxygen

19 Who proved that the planets revolve around the sun in elliptical orbits?

(A) Isaac Newton
(B) Albert Einstein
(C) Johannes Kepler
(D) Galilei Galileo

20 Which of the following is equal to one cosmic year?

(A) 365 days
(B) 24 days
(C) 2.25×10^6 days
(D) 225×10^6 years

21 Between 1979 and 1999, which of these planets was the farthest from the sun?

(A) Jupiter   (B) Neptune
(C) Uranus   (D) Mercury

22 Which is the nearest galaxy to our galaxy?

(A) Andromeda
(B) X 31
(C) Large magellanic cloud
(D) Small magellanic cloud

23 Which of the following planets takes the maximum time to rotate around itself?

(A) Mercury
(B) Pluto
(C) Venus
(D) Neptune

24 What is Halley?

(A) A comet
(B) An asteroid
(C) A satellite of Jupiter
(D) A meteorite

25 When was the sun formed?

(A) 15 billion years ago
(B) 4.5 billion years ago
(C) 10 billion years ago
(D) 11.5 billion years ago

Previous Contest Questions

1 What are stars mainly made up of?

(A) Oxygen and hydrogen
(B) Oxygen and nitrogen
(C) Hydrogen and helium
(D) Water and helium

2 Which of the following statements is *correct* about galaxies?

(A) They move towards each other.
(B) They move away from each other.
(C) They do not move at all.
(D) They have fixed number of stars.

3 Why does the pole star appear to be stationary in all seasons?

(A) It does not rotate on its axis.
(B) It happens to lie on the axis of equator.
(C) It happens to lie above the axis of north pole of the earth.
(D) It is the most distant of all the stars.

4 What makes the live telecast of a cricket match possible?

(A) Geostationary satellite
(B) Polar satellite
(C) Low-earth orbiting satellite
(D) Sun-synchronous satellite

5 Where do you find the "sea of tranquility"?

(A) On the surface of moon
(B) On the surface of earth
(C) On the surface of Mercury
(D) On the surface of Mars

6 What is a cosmic year?

(A) The time taken by the earth to revolve around the sun
(B) The time taken by the sun to revolve around itself
(C) The time taken by the earth to revolve around itself
(D) The time taken by the sun to revolve around the centre of the galaxy, the Milky Way.

7 Mercury is closer to the sun than Venus. But Venus is hotter than Mercury. Give reason.

(A) Mercury has no atmosphere and Venus has a thick atmosphere which can retain the heat.

(B) Mercury is mostly made up of sedimentary rocks while Venus contains igneous rocks.

(C) The sun absorbs the heat of the Mercury as it is closer to the sun.

(D) All of the above

8 What is the closely packed part of the comet which contains solid particles, stones and frozen water called ?

(A) Coma   (B) Nucleus
(C) Tail   (D) Orbit

9 Identify the fastest planet of the solar system.

(A) Mercury   (B) Uranus
(C) Jupiter   (D) Neptune

10 The diagram given below shows an image of a constellation used by astronomers.

What is the name of this constellation ?

(A) Orion
(B) Scorpio
(C) Big Dipper
(D) Southern cross

7. Stars and the Solar System

ACROSS

1. The natural satellite of the earth

3. Celestial bodies that revolve around the sun in great elliptical orbits

5. The nearest planet to the sun

8. Group of stars that has a recognisable shape

9. The large number of small objects that revolve around the sun

DOWN

1. Shooting stars

2. The prominent constellation in the northern sky

4. The largest planet of the solar system

6. Celestial bodies that appear to move from east to west

7. The brightest planet in the night sky

Model Test Paper

Score
25

1 Which of the following circuits gives the correct way of connecting an LED to light it up?

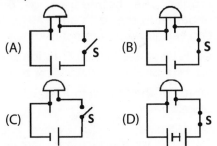

(A)   (B)   (C)   (D)

2 If the angle of incidence is 80°, what will be the angle of reflection?

(A) 80°   (B) 100°   (C) 160°   (D) 20°

3 Which of the following statements is *correct*?

(A) Rolling is easier than sliding.
(B) Sliding is easier than rolling.
(C) Dragging is easier than sliding.
(D) Dragging is easier than rolling.

4 Why does a rubber sucker stick to a surface?

(A) It is the inherent property of rubber.
(B) Gravitational force acts on it.
(C) Elastic spring force acts on it.
(D) Atmospheric pressure acts on it.

5 What is the lightning streaks that we see?

(A) UV rays from the sun
(B) Cosmic rays
(C) Accumulated electric charges
(D) IR rays from the sun

6 Which of the following frequencies cannot be heard by human beings?

(A) 1000 Hz   (B) 10,000 Hz
(C) 100 Hz   (D) 1,00,000 Hz

7 When was the sun formed?

(A) 15 billion years ago
(B) 4.5 billion years ago
(C) 10 billion years ago
(D) 11.5 billion years ago

8 Which force prevents us from slipping while walking on the road?

(A) Muscular force of our body
(B) Gravitational pull by the earth
(C) Frictional force
(D) Balanced forces of nature

9 Why are LED's extensively used to replace bulbs?

(i)	Consume less electricity
(ii)	Have longer life
(iii)	Have more power

(A) Only (i) and (ii)   (B) Only (ii) and (iii)
(C) Only (i) and (iii) (D) (i), (ii) and (iii)

10 Look at the given figure.

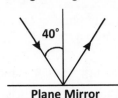

40°

Plane Mirror

Find the angle between the incident ray and the reflected ray.

(A) 60°   (B) 90°
(C) 80   (D) 40°

11 What is the purpose of an electroscope ?

(A) To detect and test small electric charges
(B) To calculate the amount of electric charge flowing through the conductor
(C) To find out the presence of antimatter
(D) To test the presence of magnetic field

12 Which of the following examples describe the change of shape on applying force?

(A) A ball being kicked
(B) A fan switched on
(C) A man jumping from a height
(D) Repeatedly tearing of a paper

13 What is the approximate height of a geostationary satellite?

(A) 6400 km   (B) 12,800 km
(C) 7200 km   (D) 36,000 km

14 Why does a meteor burn upon entering the earth's atmosphere?

(A) Due to gravitational pull
(B) Due to the heat of the earth
(C) Due to solar radiation
(D) Due to excess friction in air

15 Which of the following correctly represents the speed of sound in solids, liquids and gases in ascending order?

(A) Gas > liquid > solid
(B) Liquid > gas > solid
(C) Liquid > solid > gas
(D) Gas > liquid > gas

16 In electrolytic solutions, which of the following acts as carriers of charge?

(A) Protons   (B) Electrons
(C) Neutrons   (D) Ions

17 With what is glass coated in order to convert it into a mirror?

(A) Silver   (B) Copper
(C) Aluminium   (D) Platinum

18 Which fundamental particle in an atom has no charge?

(A) Electron   (B) Proton
(C) Neutron   (D) Both (A) and (B)

19 Which force does an archer use to pull a bow?

(A) Muscular force
(B) Magnetic force
(C) Gravitational force
(D) All of the above

20 Which of the following *correctly* describes the pitch and the frequency of the sound of a girl's scream?

(A) Low pitch, low frequency
(B) Low pitch, high frequency
(C) High pitch, low frequency
(D) High pitch, high frequency

21 What are the weak zones that are present around the boundaries of plates underneath the earth and cause slides and earthquakes commonly known as?

(A) Fault zones   (B) Eruption zones
(C) Explosive zones (D) Sliding zones

22 Which of the following is equal to one cosmic year?

(A) 365 days   (B) 24 days
(C) 2.25×10^6 days (D) 225×10^6 years

23 Why are tyres made circular in shape?

(A) It is easy to inflate circular tyres.
(B) Rolling friction is less than sliding friction.
(C) Circular tyres dissipate less heat.
(D) Circular tyres easily slow down or stop a vehicle.

24 'X' is a good conductor of electricity. Which of the following could be 'X'?

(A) Solid sodium chloride
(B) Vinegar
(C) Distilled water
(D) Liquid oxygen

25 Identify the value of persistence of vision.

(A) 1/10th of a second
(B) 1/12th of a second
(C) 1/16th of a second
(D) 1/20th of a second

Key

1	2	3	4	5	6	7	8	9	10	11	12	13	14	15	16	17	18	19	20
B	A	A	D	C	D	B	C	D	C	A	D	D	D	A	D	A	C	A	D

21	22	23	24	25
A	D	B	B	C

Synopsis

- Natural fibres like cotton are obtained from plants, while wool and silk fibres are obtained from animals.

- The rearing of silk worms for obtaining silk is called sericulture.

- Silk fibres are made up of a protein.

- Synthetic fibres are made by human beings.

- A synthetic fibre is also a chain of small units joined together. Each small unit is called a monomer and actually a chemical substance. Many such small units combine to form a large single unit called a polymer.

- Synthetic fibres are durable, less expensive and dry up fast.

- Rayon (artificial silk) is made from wood pulp while nylon is made from coal, air and water.

- Nylon by and far is the most used synthetic fibre.

- Many articles like socks, ropes, tents, parachutes, etc., are made from nylon. A nylon thread is stronger than a steel wire.

- Polyester is made up of esters which is a mixture of acid and alcohol. Polycot, polywool, terrycot, etc., are the products prepared by mixing two kinds of fibres, both artificial and natural.

- Plastic because of its mouldability finds versatile use. Thermoplastics like PVC and polythene can be remoulded, while thermosetting plastics (like bakelite and melamine) cannot be remoulded.

- Thermosetting plastics are used as kitchenware and also for electrical switches and handles.

- Plastic is non-reactive and does not corrode easily, hence it is suitable as containers of food, but are non-biodegradable. We should reduce the use of plastic.

- Waste created by plastics is not eco-friendly. The burning of plastic releases poisonous gases. Hence, these should not be disposed by burning.

- Polybags carelessly thrown are responsible for clogging the drains and also cause health problems for animals since cows and other stray animals sometimes swallow plastic bags and choke their respiratory systems.

- Use the 4R principle for the use of plastic–reduce, reuse, recycle and recover.

Multiple Choice Questions   (A) (B) (C) (D)

1. From which part of sheep is wool made from?

   (A) Skin   (B) Toes
   (C) Fleece   (D) All of the above

2. What is the process of taking out silk threads from the cocoon known as?

   (A) Rearing   (B) Sorting
   (C) Scouring   (D) Reeling

3. What do silk fibres consist of?

   (A) Vitamins   (B) Carbohydrates
   (C) Proteins   (D) Fats

4. Which of these provide compounds necessary to prepare nylon?

   | (i) Coal   (ii) Air   (iii) Water |

   (A) Only (i)
   (B) Only (i) and (ii)
   (C) Only (i) and (iii)
   (D) (i), (ii) and (iii)

5. Why is nylon useful?

   (A) It is soft, strong and light.
   (B) It is transparent, light and easy to wash.
   (C) It is strong, elastic and light.
   (D) It is soft, inexpensive and strong.

6. Which of the following statements is NOT *true*?

   (A) Fabric is made of yarn.
   (B) Jute is the outer covering of the coconut.
   (C) Polyester is a synthetic fibre.
   (D) Silk fibre is obtained from silk worms.

7. Fruits have characteristic smells. Which of these chemicals is responsible for it?

   (A) Yeast   (B) Alcohol
   (C) Cellulose   (D) Esters

8. Which of the following articles is made by using only man-made substances?

   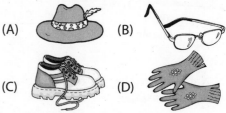

   (A)   (B)

   (C)   (D)

9. Which of the following is made from coconut fibre?

   (A) Sweaters   (B) Shoes
   (C) Mattresses   (D) Sarees

10. Which of the following statements is NOT *true*?

    (A) Polymers occur in nature.
    (B) Nylon is used in the making of parachutes.
    (C) Cellulose is made up of glucose units.
    (D) Nylon thread is weaker than cotton thread.

11. PVC is an example of

    (A) plastic.
    (B) thermoplastic.
    (C) thermosetting plastic.
    (D) acrylic.

12. Which of the following properties of plastic makes it most convenient for use?

    (A) It is non-reactive.
    (B) It is light, strong and durable.
    (C) It is easily remouldable.
    (D) All of the above

13. Which of the given materials is used to prepare synthetic fibres like polyester and acrylic?

    (A) Wood pulp   (B) Coconut fibres
    (C) Petrochemicals (D) Paper pulp

14 Match the entries in Column I with those in Column II.

	Column-I		Column-II
a	Silk	1.	Rope
b	Nylon	2.	Sweater
c	Acrylic	3.	Bottle
d	Plastic	4.	Saree

(A) a-1, b-3, c-4, d-2 (B) a-2, b-4, c-3, d-1
(C) a-3, b-1, c-4, d-2 (D) a-4, b-1, c-2, d-3

15 Which of the following is non-biodegradable?

(A) Plastic   (B) Cotton
(C) Paper   (D) Left-over food

16 By which of these processes is polythene produced?

(A) Isomerization   (B) Polymerisation
(C) Hydrogenation (D) All of the above

17 Which of the following plastic products can be remoulded?

(A) Bakelite   (B) Melamine
(C) Polythene   (D) Polycot

18 Which of the following products cannot be decomposed easily?

(A) Acrylic   (B) Polythene
(C) Plastic   (D) All of the above

19 Why is plastic coated with melamine?

(A) It becomes a good conductor of heat.

(B) It becomes strong and flexible.

(C) It becomes a fire proof plastic.

(D) It is remouldable.

20 Which of the following is used for making terylene fibres?

(A) Wood pulp   (B) Esters
(C) Acrylic   (D) Paper pulp

21 To which of the following does the 4R principle apply the most?

(A) Synthetic fibre (B) Natural fibre
(C) Metal   (D) Plastic

22 Which of the following statements is NOT *true*?

(A) Thermosetting plastics are bad conductors of heat and electricity.

(B) Thermoplastics are good conductors of heat and electricity.

(C) Plastics do not get corroded easily.

(D) Plastic is also a polymer.

23 Which of the following is a property of thermosetting plastic?

(A) Flame resistant
(B) Non-corrosive
(C) Mouldable
(D) All of the above

24 Which of the following is NOT a natural polymer?

(A) Natural rubber (B) Polyester
(C) Protein   (D) Starch

25 Which of the following fabrics is made by mixing two types of fibres?

(A) Cotton   (B) Polywool
(C) Rayon   (D) Nylon

 Previous Contest Questions

1 Which of the following is purely a synthetic fibre?

(A) Rayon   (B) Nylon
(C) Cotton   (D) Flax

2 Which of the following differences regarding thermoplastics and thermosetts is/are *true*?

	Thermoplastics	Thermosetts
(i)	Soft	Hard
(ii)	Can withstand heat	Cannot withstand heat
(iii)	No cross linkages	Cross linkages are present

(A) Only (i)
(B) Only (i) and (ii)
(C) Only (i) and (iii)
(D) (i), (ii) and (iii)

1. Synthetic Fibres and Plastics

3 Which of the following properties of nylon are most convenient for its use?

(A) It is soft, strong and heavy.
(B) It is strong, elastic and light.
(C) It is soft, inexpensive and strong.
(D) It is expensive, soft and light.

4 Which of the following is an example of a heavily cross linked polymer?

(A) Melamine   (B) Polythene
(C) Nylon   (D) Polyester

5 How does the burning of synthetic polymers such as plastic pollute the environment?

(A) By releasing smoke and toxic gases

(B) By releasing water vapour and haze

(C) By releasing water vapour and smoke

(D) By forming smog and rain

6 Which of the following is a property of thermoplastics?

(A) They do not bend.

(B) They do not get deformed easily.

(C) They are resistant to most of the chemicals.

(D) They are made up of long polymer chains with strong bonds.

7 Which of these clothes dry faster in rainy season?

(A) Cotton   (B) Wool
(C) Polyester   (D) Silk

8 Which of these clothes should you wear while cooking in the kitchen?
(A) Rayon   (B) Cotton
(C) Polyester   (D) Polycot

9 By what name is artificial (man-made) wool known as?

(A) Rayon   (B) Acrylic
(C) Polycot   (D) Polyester

10 What is the best method to avoid pollution by using plastic bags?

(A) Burying the plastic bags in the soil.

(B) Using bags made of biodegradable material.

(C) Throwing the plastic bags into the river.

(D) Burning the plastic bags in a rubbish dump.

CHAPTER 2

Materials : Metals and Non-metals

Synopsis

◆ **Metals**

❖ Metals occur in combined state or in the form of compounds.

❖ Most of the metals are solids at room temperature except mercury which is a liquid.

❖ Most of the metals have high densities because their atoms form close clusters.

❖ Most of the metals shine and can be easily polished.

❖ Metals are malleable, so they can be hammered into thin sheets. They are also ductile and hence, can be drawn into thin wires.

❖ Metals are sonorous because they produce sound when struck.

❖ Most of the metals are good conductors of heat and electricity.

❖ Metals combine with oxygen to produce basic oxides. $4Na + O_2 \rightarrow 2Na_2O$

❖ Metals react with water to form oxides and hydroxides.
$Mg + H_2O \rightarrow MgO + H_2$ and $2Na + 2H_2O \rightarrow 2NaOH + H_2$

❖ Metals react with dilute hydrochloric and sulphuric acids to produce respective salts and hydrogen.
$2Na + 2HCl \rightarrow 2NaCl + H_2$ and $2Na + H_2SO_4 \rightarrow Na_2SO_4 + H_2$

❖ Metals displace one another from their salts. $Mg + 2HCl \rightarrow MgCl_2 + H_2$

❖ Metals react with chlorine to form chlorides. $Ca + Cl_2 \rightarrow CaCl_2$

◆ **Non-metals**

❖ Non-metals occur in free state as well as in combined state.

❖ Many non-metals are solids or gases at room temperature.

❖ Non-metals look dull. Many of them are coloured.

❖ Non-metals are neither malleable nor ductile.

❖ Non-metals do not produce sound when struck.

❖ Non-metals are bad conductors of heat and electricity except graphite.

❖ Non-metals combine with oxygen to produce acidic or neutral oxides.
$2N_2 + O_2 \rightarrow 2N_2O$ and $S + O_2 \rightarrow SO_2$

❖ Non-metals cannot displace hydrogen from dilute acids and water. Thus, they do not react with them.

❖ Non-metals react with hydrogen to form covalent compounds. $H_2 + S \rightarrow H_2S$

❖ Non-metals react with chlorine to form covalent chlorides. $P_4 + 6Cl_2 \rightarrow 4PCl_3$

◆ **Corrosion of metals and its prevention**

The slow destruction of some metals by chemical reactions is called corrosion. It can be prevented by

(i)   applying paint or grease to avoid the contact with air on corrosive metals.

(ii) coating corrosive metal with non-corrosive metal.

(iii) mixing corrosive metals with non-corrosive metals by alloying.

Multiple Choice Questions

Ⓐ Ⓑ Ⓒ Ⓓ

1 How many electrons are generally present in metals in their valence shell?

(A) 1, 2 or 3   (B) 7, 8 or 9
(C) 10, 11 or 12   (D) 20, 30 or 40

2 How many electrons are present in non-metals in their outermost shell?

(A) 1, 2 or 3   (B) 8, 9 or 10
(C) 10, 20 or 30   (D) 4, 5, 6 or 7

3 To which category do antimony and arsenic belong?

(A) Metals   (B) Metalloids
(C) Non-metals   (D) Minerals

4 Identify the metal that replaces magnesium from its salt.

(A) Ca   (B) Al (C) Zn   (D) Fe

5 Aluminium foil is used for wrapping food. On which property is it used?

(A) Density   (B) Malleability
(C) Ductility   (D) Strength

6 Identify the non-metal which exhibits yellow colour.

(A) Silicon   (B) Phosphorus
(C) Sulphur   (D) Carbon

7 Which of the following are the properties of non-metals?

(i) They have low densities
(ii) They have low melting points
(iii) They are poor conductors of electricity

(A) Only (i) and (ii)
(B) Only (ii) and (iii)
(C) Only (i) and (iii)
(D) (i), (ii) and (iii)

8 Which of the following non-metals exists in liquid state at room temperature?

(A) Chlorine   (B) Nitrogen
(C) Bromine   (D) Hydrogen

9 Identify the metal that does NOT react with HCl.

(A) Ag   (B) Mg
(C) Al (D) Fe

10 Which metal reacts vigorously with HCl to produce salt and hydrogen?

(A) Na   (B) Zn
(C) Sn   (D) Pb

11 When non-metals combine with oxygen, what do they produce?

(A) Acidic oxides
(B) Basic oxides
(C) Amphoteric oxides
(D) Salts

12 Identify the oxide of a non-metal which is neutral.

(A) SO_2 (B) NO_2
(C) P_2O_3 (D) CO

13 Phosphorus combines with oxygen to form oxides. How many types of oxides are formed by it?

(A) One   (B) Two
(C) Three   (D) Four

14 Which of the following dissolves in water to form sulphuric acid?

(A) Sulphur dioxide
(B) Sulphur
(C) Sulphur trioxide
(D) Copper sulphate

15 Which of the following compounds is used to make photographic films?

(A) Sodium chloride
(B) Silver bromide
(C) Potassium iodide
(D) Copper chloride

16 Which material is used for making crucibles?

(A) Sulphur   (B) Silicon
(C) Graphite   (D) Phosphorus

17 Which non-metal is used in the treatment of rubber during the process of vulcani-sation?

(A) Sulphur   (B) Phosphorus
(C) Carbon   (D) Chlorine

18 Which of the following is called a noble metal?

(A) Mercury   (B) Gold
(C) Lithium   (D) Caesium

19 Identify the metal which is soft.
(A) Na   (B) Pb   (C) Al   (D) Cu

20 Why is tungsten used as a filament in electric bulbs?

(A) It is sonorous.
(B) It is metallic.
(C) It has a high melting point.
(D) It has high density.

21 Which of the following is NOT a heavy metal?

(A) Cd   (B) Hg   (C) Pb   (D) K

22 Which of the following substances will prevent corrosion of metals?

(A) Nitrogen   (B) Hydrogen
(C) Oxygen   (D) Carbon

23 Which of the following metals in their molten state cause galvanisation of an iron article?

(A) Zinc   (B) Copper
(C) Carbon   (D) Gold

24 Arrange the given metals in the descending order of their reactivity.

(A) Aluminium, copper, potassium
(B) Sodium, iron, copper
(C) Silver, zinc, calcium
(D) Magnesium, copper, sodium

25 When a little aluminium powder is added to dilute sulphuric acid, the product(s) formed in the reaction is

(A) sulphur dioxide.
(B) aluminium sulphate.
(C) hydrogen.
(D) Both (B) and (C)

Previous Contest Questions

1 Which of the following statements is true of the given chemical reactions?

$$ZnO + C \rightarrow Zn + CO$$
$$2Fe_3O_3 + 3C \rightarrow 6Fe + 3CO_2$$

(A) Carbon is reduced.
(B) Carbon is oxidised.
(C) Metal oxide is reduced to metal.
(D) Metal oxide is oxidised.

2 Why is gold mixed with copper?

(A) To make gold soft
(B) To make gold hard
(C) To make gold more yellowish
(D) To give gold a lustre

3 Which of the following statements is *correct*?

(A) All metals are ductile .
(B) All non-metals are ductile.
(C) Generally, metals are ductile.
(D) Some non-metals are ductile.

4 Study the reaction given below.

$$X + YSO_4 \rightarrow Y + XSO_4$$

What are 'X' and 'Y' ?

(A) Al, Mg   (B) Zn, Cu
(C) Ag, K   (D) H, Al

5 Which of the following is NOT a general property of metals?

(A) Ductility
(B) Malleability
(C) Bad conductor of electricity
(D) Sonorous nature

6 Which of the following is a chemical displacement reaction?

(A) $2Al + Fe_2O_3 \xrightarrow{heat} Al_2O_3 + 2Fe + Heat$

(B) $2Na + Cl_2 \longrightarrow 2NaCl$

(C) $P_2O_5 + 3H_2O \longrightarrow 2H_3PO_4$

(D) $2PbS + 3O_2 \xrightarrow{heat} PbO + 3SO_2$

7 Which of the following statements is NOT true of sodium and potassium?

(A) Both are metals.

(B) Both are hard.

(C) Both are solids at room temperature.

(D) Both react with oxygen to form oxides.

8 Identify the true statement from the following.

(A) Metals have fixed melting points whereas non-metals do not.

(B) All metals are malleable.

(C) The hardest substance known is a non-metal.

(D) Tungsten is a bad conductor of heat and electricity.

9 Which of the following metals does NOT produce hydrogen gas when added to acid?

(A) Potassium   (B) Gold
(C) Zinc   (D) Magnesium

10 Metal 'X' reacts very slowly with water but reacts vigorously with steam. Identify metal 'X'.

(A) Magnesium   (B) Silver
(C) Copper   (D) Potassium

CROSSWORD

1. Synthetic Fibres and Plastics

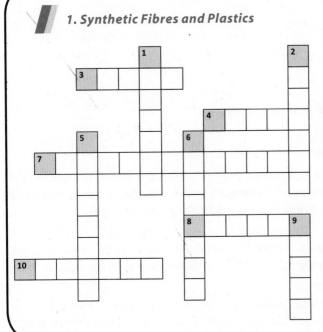

ACROSS

3. It is also known as artificial silk

4. Material used in making floppy disks

7. The kind of plastic for which PVC is an example

8. Coating used in non-stick pans

10. Material used in the making of T-shirts

DOWN

1. A mixture of polyester and cotton

2. Materials obtained from natural or artificial sources by weaving the fibre

5. A kind of plastic used in floor tiles

6. Materials that are non-biodegradable

9. Man-made fibre prepared from coal, water and air

2. Materials : Metals and Non-metals

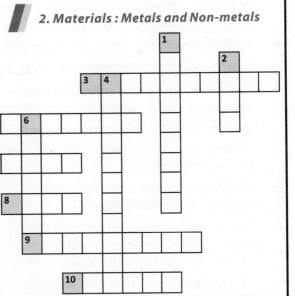

ACROSS

3. The category to which antimony, and arsenic belong

5. Gas liberated in the reaction of zinc with HCl gas

7. Alloy containing Cu and Zn, used for making utensils

8. One of the noble metals

9. The ability of a metal to be drawn into wires

10. Reactant that gives metal oxides in a reaction with metals

DOWN

1. Characteristic of metals that enables them to be hammered into thin sheets

2. Element used in the galvanising of iron

4. Something that is conducted through metals

6. Hardest substance known

Coal and Petroleum

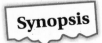

Synopsis

◆ **Sources of energy:**

All sources of energy can be divided into two categories:

(1) renewable sources of energy and

(2) non-renewable sources of energy.

◆ **Renewable sources of energy:** The sources of energy which are found in nature and inexhaustible are called renewable sources of energy. Some renewable sources of energy are solar energy, geothermal energy, wind energy, tidal energy, bio-energy.

◆ **Non-renewable sources of energy:** The sources of energy which have accumulated in nature over a long period of time and cannot be quickly replaced once exhausted are called non-renewable sources of energy. Some non-renewable sources of energy are fossil fuels like coal, petroleum, natural gas.

◆ **Coal and its products:** Coal is a complex mixture of elements like carbon, hydrogen and oxygen. Coal is formed by the process of carbonisation. Coal is one of the cheapest and widely used fuels. Anthracite, bituminous, lignite and peat are different varieties of coal. The most important variety of coal which is used as a fuel is bituminous coal. The process of heating coal in the absence of air is called destructive distillation. Destructive distillation of coal gives products like coal gas, ammonical liquor, coal tar and coke.

◆ Coke obtained from coal is used to make fuel gases like water gas and producer gas.

◆ Coal tar is a black, thick liquid with an unpleasant smell.

◆ Coal gas is a mixture of hydrogen, methane and carbon monoxide.

◆ **Petroleum and its products:** Economy of a nation depends, to a great extent, on its petroleum wealth. That is why petroleum is called 'Black Gold'.

◆ Crude oil is a complex mixture of solid, liquid and gaseous hydrocarbons mixed with water, salt and other particles.

◆ Petroleum is lighter than water and insoluble in it. Petroleum is a dark coloured, viscous and a strong smelling liquid.

◆ Petroleum is extracted by drilling holes in the earth's crust, sinking pipes and pumping out the oil. Petroleum is then refined by fractional distillation. Important fractions of petroleum are gasoline, kerosene, diesel, lubricating oil, petrol, etc.

◆ Coal and petroleum resources are limited, so we should use them judiciously.

◆ **Natural gas:** Natural gas is stored under high pressure as CNG which is used for power generation and fuel. It is a cleaner fuel and less polluting. It consists mainly of methane (85%), ethane (10%), propane (3%) and others.

Multiple Choice Questions   (A) (B) (C) (D)

1 Which of the following is a fossil fuel?

(A) Petroleum   (B) Wood
(C) Cow dung   (D) Dry leaves

2 Where does natural gas occur?

(A) Above petroleum oil
(B) Below petroleum oil
(C) Along with petroleum oil
(D) Inside volcanic mountains

3 What is the common name of petroleum?

(A) Black gold   (B) Yellow gold
(C) Green gold   (D) Blue gold

4 What are the most common sources of energy used in automobiles?

(A) Wood and coal
(B) Petroleum and diesel
(C) LPG and cow dung
(D) Natural gas and coal

5 When an oil well is drilled through rocks, which of the following comes out first?
(A) Coal gas
(B) Marsh gas
(C) Natural gas
(D) Carbon dioxide

6 By what process is petroleum refined?

(A) Fractional distillation
(B) Destructive distillation
(C) Distillation
(D) All of the above

7 During fractional distillation, the crude petroleum is heated to

(A) 600 °C.   (B) 400-500 °C.
(C) 200 °C.   (D) 100 °C.

8 Identify the fuel that leaves more smoke and ash on burning.

(A) Solid fuels
(B) Liquid fuels
(C) Gaseous fuels
(D) Any one of the above

9 What is the underlying principle based on which fractional distillation is carried out?

(A) Different densities of each fraction

(B) Different molecular weights of each fraction

(C) Different boiling points of each fraction

(D) Different melting points of each fraction

10 Which of the following is used as a fuel?
(A) Gasoline   (B) Ether
(C) Tar   (D) Grease

11 By which of the given processes is coal formed?

(A) Carbonisation (B) Distillation
(C) Vapourisation (D) Evaporation

12 Which of the following has the lowest percentage of carbon?

(A) Lignite   (B) Bituminous
(C) Anthracite   (D) Peat

13 Which of the forms of coal has the highest percentage of carbon?

(A) Anthracite   (B) Bituminous
(C) Peat   (D) Lignite

14 What do fuels combine with to produce heat and light?

(A) CO_2 (B) CO
(C) H_2 (D) O_2

15 What does natural gas **mainly** consist of?

(A) C_2H_6 (B) CH_4
(C) C_3H_8 (D) C_4H_{10}

16 What does gobar gas produced from animal and plant waste contain?

(A) Ethane   (B) Methane
(C) Propane   (D) Acetylene

17 In LPG cylinder, how is the gas liquified?
   (A) By increasing volume
   (B) By applying high pressure
   (C) By increasing temperature
   (D) By reducing pressure

18 In fractional distillation of petroleum, where do the vapours with highest boiling point condense?
   (A) In the upper-most portion
   (B) In the lower-most portion
   (C) In the middle portion
   (D) Cannot be said

19 Why is kerosene oil regarded more suitable than petrol in oil lamps?
   (A) Kerosene is heavier.
   (B) Kerosene is expensive.
   (C) Kerosene is less volatile.
   (D) Kerosene is more volatile.

20 Where is kerosene mainly used?
   (A) In laying down roads.
   (B) As fuel in jet engines.
   (C) In making water proof materials.
   (D) In furnaces of industries.

21 Match the entries in Column I with those in Column II.

	Column-I		Column-II
a.	Carbonisation	1.	Coke
b.	Destructive distillation	2.	Coal
c.	Cracking	3.	Petroleum
d.	Refining	4.	Hydrocarbons

   (A) a-1, b-2, c-3, d-4
   (B) a-2, b-1, c-4, d-3
   (C) a-3, b-2, c-4, d-1
   (D) a-4, b-3, c-2, d-1

22 Which of these is the main constituent of petroleum gas?
   (A) Butane   (B) Propane
   (C) Methane   (D) Ethane

23 What is the source of fly ash?
   (A) Petroleum   (B) Natural gas
   (C) Coal   (D) All of the above

24 Which one of the following is NOT a fossil fuel?
   (A) Coal   (B) Biogas
   (C) Petroleum   (D) Natural gas

25 Study the characteristics given below:

   Ʊ It is a tough, porous and black substance.
   Ʊ It is a pure form of carbon.

   Based on the above characteristics, identify it from the following.
   (A) Kerosene   (B) Petrol
   (C) Coke   (D) Lubricating oil

Previous Contest Questions

1 Which of the following statements is *true* about petroleum?
   (A) Lighter than water and soluble in it.
   (B) Heavier than water and insoluble in it.
   (C) Lighter than water and insoluble in it.
   (D) Heavier than water and soluble in it.

2 Which of the following properties is NOT a characteristic of a good fuel?
   (A) High ignition temperature
   (B) Low cost
   (C) Causes minimum pollution
   (D) Readily available

3 Why is producer gas not a good fuel?
   (A) It contains CO which is poisonous.
   (B) It contains CO_2 which is abundant.
   (C) It contains CO_2 which does not burn.
   (D) It contains N_2 which does not burn.

4 Which of the following is most harmful for the human body?
   (A) CO
   (B) CO_2
   (C) Oxides of nitrogen
   (D) Lead compounds

5 What are the characteristics of a rocket fuel?
   (A) Light and compact
   (B) High calorific value
   (C) Burns rapidly
   (D) All of the above

6 Which of the following is formed during the process of anaerobic fermentation?

(A) Biogas   (B) Natural gas
(C) Water gas   (D) Petroleum

7 Which of the following has the highest boiling point?

(A) Kerosene   (B) Petrol
(C) Diesel   (D) Water

8 How is coke superior than coal as a fuel?

(A) Coal is a mineral and burns releasing smoke while coke is a residue.

(B) Coal is an impure form of carbon, while coke is a pure form of carbon.

(C) Only coal consists of atoms of carbon, hydrogen, oxygen and sulphur while coke mainly consists of carbon.

(D) All of the above

9 Which of the following is in descending order of the quality of coal?

(A) Peat > bituminous > lignite > anthracite

(B) Bituminous > peat > lignite > anthracite

(C) Anthracite > bituminous > lignite > peat

(D) Lignite > anthracite > bituminous > peat

10 Which of the following is an example of a liquid fuel?

(A) Paraffin wax   (B) Coal gas
(C) L.P.G.   (D) Alcohol

✧ ✧ ✧

Combustion and Flame

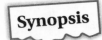

♦ **Fuels**

Substances which are burnt to produce heat energy are known as fuels. Fuels can be in the form of solid, liquid or gas. Gaseous fuels are better than liquid fuels due to the highest calorific value. Liquids in turn have more calorific value than solid fuels. The main gaseous fuels are natural gas, producer gas, water gas, L.P.G and biogas. L.P.G is a mixture of two hydrocarbons – butane and isobutane. The advantages of L.P.G are

(i) high calorific value.

(ii) burns with a smokeless flame.

(iii) does not produce any poisonous gases on burning.

♦ **Calorific value of fuel**

The amount of heat produced by burning 1 g of fuel completely is known as its calorific value.

♦ **Characteristics of an ideal fuel**

An ideal fuel should be cheap, readily available, combustible, easy to transport and store, safe and should have a high calorific value.

♦ **Combustion**

It is an oxidation reaction which is accompanied by the evolution of heat and light. Paper, kerosene, petrol, straw, etc. are combustible substances. Iron, glass and diamond are non-combustible. The lowest temperature at which a substance starts burning is called its ignition temperature.

♦ **Conditions necessary for combustion are**

(i)   the presence of combustible substance,

(ii) the presence of supporter of combustion (oxygen),

(iii) the attainment of ignition temperature.

♦ **Types of combustion**

(i)   If combustion of a substance takes place with high speed, it is known as rapid combustion. **e.g.,** candle starts burning when a burning matchstick is brought near its wick.

(ii) The combustion in which no external heat is supplied to the substance is known as spontaneous combustion. **e.g.,** burning of white phosphorus in air.

(iii) The combustion in which large amounts of gases are evolved with the production of large amounts of heat, light and sound by a substance is called explosion. **e.g.,** burning of crackers.

Multiple Choice Questions

A B C D

1 What are the two main hydrocarbons present in L.P.G.?

(A) Butane + propane
(B) Butane + isobutane
(C) Propane + ethane
(D) Methane + ethane

2 What is the heat produced by burning 1 g of fuel completely known as?

(A) Heat capacity
(B) Calorific value
(C) Vapour density
(D) Boiling point

3 Which of the following has the highest calorific value?

(A) Petrol   (B) Coke
(C) Natural gas   (D) Kerosene

4 Which of the following has the characteristics of a good fuel?

(A) Coke   (B) Butane
(C) Coal   (D) Kerosene

5 What is burning of a substance in the presence of air with the evolution of heat called?

(A) Distillation   (B) Carbonisation
(C) Combustion   (D) Refining

6 When methane burns in air, what are the products formed?

(A) $CO_2 + 2H_2O$ + heat
(B) $CO_2 + H_2$
(C) $CO + O_2$
(D) $CO_2 + O_2$ + heat

7 What kind of reaction is combustion?

(A) Reduction   (B) Redox
(C) Substitution   (D) Oxidation

8 Which of the following is a non-combustible substance?

(A) Coke   (B) Diamond
(C) Coal   (D) Wood

9 What is the lowest temperature at which a substance starts burning called?

(A) Minimum temperature
(B) Maximum temperature
(C) Boiling temperature
(D) Ignition temperature

10 If the temperature falls below its ignition temperature, then what happens to the burning substance?

(A) It gets extinguished.
(B) It burns brightly.
(C) It burns dimly.
(D) It burns with smoke.

11 Which of the following is an example of rapid combustion?

(A) Candle
(B) Cracker
(C) White phosphorus
(D) Sulphur

12 In which of the following types of combustion are heat, light and sound produced?

(A) Rapid   (B) Explosive
(C) Spontaneous   (D) All of the above

13 Match the entries in Column-I with those in Column-II correctly.

	Column-I		Column-II
a.	Dark inner zone	1.	Hottest part (No carbon)
b.	Blue zone	2.	Partial combustion
c.	Luminous zone	3.	Unburnt vapours of wax
d.	Non-luminous zone	4.	Complete combustion

(A) a-1, b-2, c-3, d-4
(B) a-2, b-3, c-4, d-1
(C) a-3, b-4, c-2, d-1
(D) a-4, b-1, c-2, d-3

4. Combustion and Flame

14 What does the blue zone in an L.P.G. flame indicate?

(A) Unburnt vapours
(B) Partial decomposition
(C) Moderately hot
(D) Hottest zone of complete combustion

15 What does natural gas contain?

(A) Methane, ethane, propane.
(B) Butane, propane and ethane.
(C) Pentene, methane and ethylene.
(D) Hexane, butane and ethane.

16 How is synthetic petrol produced?

(A) From petroleum   (B) From wood
(C) From coal   (D) From L.P.G.

17 Arrange the following fuels in the increasing order of their calorific value.

(i) Petrol	(ii) Wood
(iii) Coal	(iv) Natural gas

(A) (i), (ii), (iii), (iv)
(B) (ii), (iii), (iv) and (i)
(C) (ii), (i), (iii) and (iv)
(D) (ii), (iii), (i) and (iv)

18 What does the incomplete combustion of a fuel give?

(A) CO   (B) CO_2
(C) SO_2 (D) Oxides of nitrogen

19 The total amount of heat produced by a fuel having a calorific value of 20 kJ kg^{-1} was found to be 50,000 joules. How much fuel was burnt?

(A) 2500 kg   (B) 250 kg
(C) 25 kg   (D) 2.5 kg

20 What is combustion?

(A) An exothermic reaction
(B) An endothermic reaction
(C) A displacement reaction
(D) A reduction reaction

21 Inspite of the danger involved with hydrogen, it is used for some applications. Where is it used?

(A) Rocket fuel
(B) Oxyhydrogen flame
(C) Car fuel
(D) All of the above

22 A family consumes 12 kg of L.P.G. in 30 days. Calculate the average energy consumed per day, if the calorific value of L.P.G. is 50 kJ kg^{-1}.

(A) 10,000 J per day
(B) 15,000 J per day
(C) 20,000 J per day
(D) 25,000 J per day

23 What ignition temperature does an inflammable substance have?

(A) More than 100 °C
(B) Less than 100 °C
(C) More than 200 °C
(D) Between 200 °C to 350 °C

24 What is the disadvantage of incomplete combustion of a fuel?

(A) Unburnt carbon gets released.
(B) Air gets polluted.
(C) Respiratory problems arise.
(D) All of the above

25 Which of the following is the best extinguisher for inflammable materials?

(A) Water
(B) Sulphur dioxide
(C) Carbon dioxide
(D) Carbon monoxide

Previous Contest Questions

1 On which of these factors does the flame produced by a fuel depend upon?

(A) Calorific value
(B) Amount of oxygen
(C) The chemical composition of a fuel
(D) All of the above

2   Which of the following statements is NOT true?

(A) CO_2 is the best fire extinguisher.

(B) Global warming can cause acid rain.

(C) Burning of coal and diesel releases sulphur dioxide gas.

(D) L.P.G. has higher calorific value than biogas.

3   Why is L.P.G, used as domestic fuel, mixed with a strong smelling volatile liquid like mercaptan?

(A) For better combustion

(B) For good smell/fragrance

(C) For detection of gas leakage

(D) For higher calorific value

4   Hydrogen gas has the highest calorific value i.e., 150 kJ kg^{-1}, yet it is not used as a fuel. Why?

(A) It is explosive in nature.

(B) It causes storage problem.

(C) It causes transportation problem.

(D) All of the above

5   When wood is used as a fuel in chullahs, gaps are left in between logs of wood. Why is it done so?

(A) To facilitate movement of air

(B) To prevent more consumption of wood

(C) To control temperature

(D) All of these

6   For a spontaneous combustion to take place, which condition given below is necessary?

(A) Flame
(B) Low ignition temperature
(C) Rise in temperature
(D) Temperature below 30 °C

7   An electric spark is struck between two electrodes placed near each other, inside a closed tank full of petrol. What will happen?

(A) Spontaneous combustion of petrol
(B) Explosion
(C) Slow combustion of petrol
(D) Nothing will happen

8   One gram of which of these will give out the maximum amount of heat by complete combustion?

(A) Wood   (B) Coal
(C) Diesel   (D) Biogas

9   What are the essential requirements for a fire to start and continue?

| (i) Fuel |
| (ii) Air (oxygen) |
| (iii) Heat |

(A) Only (i) and (ii)

(B) Only (ii) and (iii)

(C) Only (i) and (iii)

(D) (i), (ii) and (iii)

10 Which of the following statements is NOT true?

(A) Spontaneous combustion takes place without any apparent cause.

(B) The luminous zone of a flame has high temperature.

(C) Carbon dioxide gas causes global warming.

(D) The calorific value of a fuel is expressed in kJ/kg^{-1}.

CROSSWORD

3. Coal and Petroleum

ACROSS

4. Fuel for jet air crafts
6. These fuels are formed from the dead. remains of living organisms
7. Fuel for home and industry
8. A cleaner fuel in transport vehicles

DOWN

1. Petrol and diesel are obtained from this natural resource
2. Pure form of carbon
3. Solvent for dry cleaning
5. Used for road surfacing

4. Combustion and Flame

ACROSS

3. Something that is caused when ignition temperature is the lowest
4. A chemical process in which a substance reacts with oxygen to give off heat
5. A type of chemical process in which a material suddenly bursts into flames
7. A substance when burnt produces light and heat.
8. Reaction in which a large amount of gas and light/heat is formed

DOWN

1. The consequence of cutting down of trees
2. The substance that can undergo combustion
6. A type of chemical process where the fuel burns quickly and produces heat and light

Pollution of Air and Water

Synopsis

◆ Pollution is the introduction of harmful substances into the environment, which can harm the health, survival or activities of living organisms. Pollutants may be biodegradable or non-biodegradable. Biodegradable pollutants can be broken down by biological agents, whereas non-biodegradable pollutants cannot be broken down by any agents and remain in the environment for a long time.

◆ The major causes of air pollution are industries and automobiles. The burning of fossil fuels releases carbon dioxide, carbon monoxide, sulphur dioxide, oxides of nitrogen, hydrocarbons and particulate matter. Industrial processes release polluting gases and particulate matter.

◆ The oxides of nitrogen and sulphur combine with rainwater to form acid rain, which affects soil fertility, vegetation, buildings and monuments.

◆ Carbon dioxide and some other gases, like methane are called greenhouse gases. They trap radiations from the earth and are considered to be the cause of global warming.

◆ Air pollution can be reduced by modifying automobile engines, using CNG in the place of petrol or diesel, using unleaded petrol, removing pollutants from industrial waste gases before their release into the atmosphere and using cleaner sources of energy.

◆ Water pollution can be classified into two types - chemical and biological.

◆ Chemical pollution of water is caused by the discharge of unwanted chemicals into water bodies.

◆ Biological pollution of water bodies is caused by oxygen-demanding wastes and disease-causing micro-organisms.

◆ The major causes of water pollution are industrial effluents and urban sewage. Disease-causing organisms, agricultural and industrial chemicals, oxygen-demanding organic wastes and hot water are some of the major categories of pollutants.

◆ The accumulation of plant nutrients in water bodies enhances the rapid growth of algae. The algae cut off the supply of light to organisms and their decomposition by bacteria uses up dissolved oxygen from water.

◆ Eutrophication is an increase in the rate of supply of organic matter in an ecosystem.

◆ Water pollution can be prevented or reduced by the treatment of sewage, treatment of industrial wastes, limited use of pesticides and fertilisers, burning of hospital wastes and proper disposal of dead bodies.

◆ Water fit for drinking is called potable water.

◆ Alum facilitates the removal of suspended particles from water by sedimentation.

◆ Water can be disinfected by boiling, chlorination, ozonisation or irradiation with ultraviolet rays.

◆ Sustainable development implies a change in all aspects of life. The public must be educated on the 3Rs concept, that is recycle, reuse and reduce to conserve and preserve resources.

Multiple Choice Questions   A   B   C   D

1 The pie chart given below shows the composition of different gases in air.

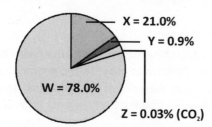

X = 21.0%
Y = 0.9%
W = 78.0%
Z = 0.03% (CO_2)

Identify gases W, X and Y.

	W	X	Y
(A)	Nitrogen	Rare gases	Oxygen
(B)	Carbon	Oxygen	Rare gases
(C)	Nitrogen	Oxygen	Rare gases
(D)	Rare gases	Hydrogen	Oxygen

2 Which of the following air pollutants is wrongly matched with the effect it causes?

(A) Dust - reduces photosynthesis in green plants.

(B) Carbon monoxide - reduces oxygen in the blood.

(C) Chlorofluorocarbons - damages nerves and tissues.

(D) Nicotine - hardens and narrows blood vessels.

3 Which of the following does NOT cause air pollution?

(A) Increasing forest reserves
(B) Using pesticides in farms
(C) Developing housing estates
(D) Quarrying for limestone

4 Which of the following is NOT a general pollutant of atmosphere?

(A) CO_2 (B) SO_2
(C) SO_3 (D) NO_2

5 Identify the gas associated with greenhouse effect.

(A) Carbon dioxide
(B) Oxygen
(C) Nitrogen dioxide
(D) Sulphur dioxide

6 What is the outcome of the release of carbon particles and smoke from factories?

(A) Increases the rate of respiration in plants.

(B) Decreases the rate of photosynthesis in plants.

(C) Increases the absorption of carbon dioxide by plants.

(D) Decreases the rate of transpiration in plants.

7 Which of the following gases can result in the formation of acid rain?

(A) Ozone
(B) Carbon monoxide
(C) Sulphur dioxide
(D) Chlorofluorocarbon

8 Heat is reflected from the earth's surface and trapped in the atmosphere. Which phenomena is being referred to?

(A) Global warming
(B) Ozone depletion
(C) Greenhouse effect
(D) Thermal pollution

9 Which of the water pollutants is INCORRECTLY paired with the source?

(A) Oil spill – ship
(B) Pesticide – oil palm plantation
(C) Sewage – factories
(D) Nitrate – farm

10 Which of the following gases is regarded as an atmospheric pollutant?

(A) O_2 (B) O_3 (C) SO_2 (D) N_2

11 What is the effect of sulphur dioxide present in air on human beings?

(A) Harms the skin and the lungs

(B) Mixes with the blood and prevents it from carrying oxygen

(C) Affects the heart and the liver

(D) Raises the air temperature

12 How are lead particles released into the air?

(A) By burning coal in thermal power stations

(B) By burning petrol in automobiles

(C) By burning biomass in chullahs

(D) By burning LPG for cooking

13 From which of the following bad effects does the ozone layer in our atmosphere protect us?

(A) Carbon dioxide
(B) CFC's
(C) The sun's ultraviolet rays
(D) All of the above

14 How are monuments of marble destroyed?

(A) By sulphur dioxide pollution.
(B) By carbon monoxide pollution.
(C) By pesticide pollution.
(D) By dust particles.

15 Which of the major sources of air pollution contributes pollutants like chlorofluorohydrocarbons?

(A) Industrial effluents
(B) Aerosols
(C) Sewage pollutants
(D) All of the above

16 Which of these is the major air pollutant in cities like Delhi and Kolkata?

(A) Carbon monoxide
(B) Hydrocarbons
(C) Suspended particulate matter
(D) Oxides of nitrogen

17 Which of the following applications use catalytic converters?

(A) Automobiles (B) Wind mills
(C) Poultry farms (D) Dairy farms

18 What is smog?

(A) A combination of fire and water.
(B) A combination of smoke and fog.
(C) A combination of water and smoke.
(D) A combination of air and water.

19 If there is no CO_2 in the atmosphere, what would happen to the earth's temperature?

(A) It would be less than the present.
(B) It would be the same as present.
(C) It would be higher than the present.
(D) It depends on the O_2 content of air.

20 Which of the following is NOT a feature of potable water?

(A) Clean, colourless and odourless

(B) Free from bacteria

(C) Have excessive sodium, calcium and magnesium

(D) Having dissolved oxygen and carbon dioxide

21 Which of the following pollutants is NOT present in the vehicular exhaust emissions?

(A) Lead
(B) Ammonia
(C) Carbon monoxide
(D) Particulate matter

22 What is the main cause of pollution of water in India?

(A) Discharge of untreated sewage
(B) Bathing
(C) Discharge of industrial waste
(D) Both (A) and (C)

23 In which part of atmosphere is ozone layer present?

(A) Stratosphere (B) Troposphere
(C) Mesosphere (D) Thermosphere

24 What is the main cause of sulphur dioxide emissions?

(A) Agricultural farms
(B) Petroleum refineries
(C) Thermal Power plants
(D) Water resources

25 Which of these steps when adopted will contribute towards better waste management?

(A) Reduce the amount of waste formed
(B) Reuse the waste
(C) Recycle the waste
(D) All of the above

Previous Contest Questions

1 Which of the following, will NOT help in reducing air pollution?

(A) Burn household rubbish in incinerators.
(B) Use catalytic converters in motor vehicles.
(C) Fix electric precipitators to factory chimneys.
(D) Ban smoking in public places such as in cinema theatres.

2 Which of the following is due to global warming?

(i) An increase in the water level in the sea
(ii) The melting of snow on mountain peaks
(iii) A decrease in food production by plants

(A) Only (i) and (ii)
(B) Only (ii) and (iii)
(C) Only (i) and (iii)
(D) (i), (ii) and (iii)

3 Which of these is the bio-indicator of air pollution?

(A) Algae   (B) Ferns
(C) Mushrooms   (D) Lichens

4 What does the term 'conserving the environment' mean?

(A) Not allowing man and animal from using natural resources
(B) Not lowering the quality of the environment
(C) Changing natural resources from their original state
(D) Preserving nature that has been destroyed

5 How can pollution from the burning of fossil fuels be reduced?

(i) By using an incinerator.
(ii) By using renewable sources of energy.
(iii) By fixing catalytic converters in vehicles.

(A) Only (i) and (ii)
(B) Only (ii) and (iii)
(C) Only (i) and (iii)
(D) (i), (ii) and (iii)

6 What is caused, if carbon dioxide is released into the air?

(A) Acid rain
(B) Eutrophication
(C) Global warming
(D) Respiratory problems

7 How is sewage water purified for recycling?

(A) By the action of fish.
(B) By the action of microorganisms.
(C) By the action of fuels.
(D) By the action of non-biodegradable chemicals.

8 What is the trapping of heat radiations by earth's atmosphere known as?

(A) Global warming
(B) Marble cancer
(C) Greenhouse effect
(D) Ozone hole

9 What are the effects of discharging excess heat from electrical power stations into rivers and lakes?

> (i)   The biological oxygen demand value of the water decreases
> (ii) Instant death of certain organisms
> (iii) The population of algae increases
> (iv) The concentration of dissolved oxygen increases

(A) Only (i) and (ii)
(B) Only (ii) and (iii)
(C) Only (i), (ii) and (iii)
(D) Only (i), (ii) and (iv)

10 Which of the following is NOT an air pollutant?

(A) N_2
(B) N_2O
(C) NO
(D) CO

5. Pollution of Air and Water

ACROSS

5. Contamination of natural resources by substances harmful to life

6. One of the most precious and abundant natural resources

7. Impurities in water

8. The major constituent of air

DOWN

1. The gas that causes global warming when its levels increase

2. Water fit for drinking

3. Constituent of air that supports life

4. Unwanted particles in air or water

Model Test Paper

Score

25

1 Which of these steps when adopted will contribute towards better waste management?

(A) Reduce the amount of waste formed
(B) Reuse the waste
(C) Recycle the waste
(D) All of the above

2 In LPG cylinder, how is the gas liquified?

(A) By increasing volume
(B) By applying high pressure
(C) By increasing temperature
(D) By reducing pressure

3 PVC is an example of

(A) plastic.
(B) thermoplastic.
(C) thermosetting plastic.
(D) acrylic.

4 Identify the metal that does NOT react with HCl.

(A) Ag (B) Mg (C) Al (D) Fe

5 Which of the following is the best extinguisher for inflammable materials?

(A) Water
(B) Sulphur dioxide
(C) Carbon dioxide
(D) Carbon monoxide

6 Which of these provide compounds necessary to prepare nylon?

(i) Coal	(ii) Air	(iii) Water

(A) Only (i)   (B) Only (i) and (ii)
(C) Only (i) and (iii) (D) (i), (ii) and (iii)

7 Arrange the given metals in the descending order of their reactivity.

(A) Aluminium, copper, potassium
(B) Sodium, iron, copper
(C) Silver, zinc, calcium
(D) Magnesium, copper, sodium

8 Which of the forms of coal has the highest percentage of carbon?

(A) Anthracite   (B) Bituminous
(C) Peat   (D) Lignite

9 Arrange the following fuels in the increasing order of their calorific value.

(i) Petrol	(ii) Wood
(iii) Coal	(iv) Natural gas

(A) (i), (ii), (iii), (iv)
(B) (ii), (iii), (iv) and (i)
(C) (ii), (i), (iii) and (iv)
(D) (ii), (iii), (i) and (iv)

10 From which of the following bad effects does the ozone layer in our atmosphere protect us?

(A) Carbon dioxide
(B) CFC's
(C) The sun's ultraviolet rays
(D) All of the above

11 Which of the following is non-biodegradable?

(A) Plastic   (B) Cotton
(C) Paper   (D) Left-over food

12 If the temperature falls below its ignition temperature, then what happens to the burning substance?

(A) It gets extinguished.
(B) It burns brightly.
(C) It burns dimly.
(D) It burns with smoke.

13 What are the most common sources of energy used in automobiles?

(A) Wood and coal
(B) Petroleum and diesel
(C) LPG and cow dung
(D) Natural gas and coal

14 What is the underlying principle based on which fractional distillation is carried out?

(A) Different densities of each fraction
(B) Different molecular weights of each fraction
(C) Different boiling points of each fraction
(D) Different melting points of each fraction

15 Phosphorus combines with oxygen to form oxides. How many types of oxides are formed by it?

(A) One   (B) Two
(C) Three   (D) Four

16 Which of the following is NOT a general pollutant of atmosphere?

(A) CO_2 (B) SO_2 (C) SO_3 (D) NO_2

17 Which material is used for making crucibles?

(A) Sulphur   (B) Silicon
(C) Graphite   (D) Phosphorus

18 A family consumes 12 kg of L.P.G. in 30 days. Calculate the average energy consumed per day, if the calorific value of L.P.G. is 50 kJ kg^{-1}.

(A) 10,000 J per day
(B) 15,000 J per day
(C) 20,000 J per day
(D) 25,000 J per day

19 Why is plastic coated with melamine?

(A) It becomes a good conductor of heat.
(B) It becomes strong and flexible
(C) It becomes a fire proof plastic.
(D) It is remouldable.

20 Which of the major sources of air pollution contributes pollutants like chlorofluorohydrocarbons?

(A) Industrial effluents
(B) Aerosols
(C) Sewage pollutants
(D) All of the above

21 Which of the following is made from coconut fibre?

(A) Sweaters   (B) Shoes
(C) Mattresses   (D) Sarees

22 Which of the following substances will prevent corrosion of metals?

(A) Nitrogen   (B) Hydrogen
(C) Oxygen   (D) Carbon

23 By which of the given processes is coal formed?

(A) Carbonisation (B) Distillation
(C) Vapourisation (D) Evaporation

24 When methane burns in air, what are the products formed?

(A) $CO_2 + 2H_2O + heat$
(B) $CO_2 + H_2$
(C) $CO + O_2$
(D) $CO_2 + O_2 + heat$

25 Which of the following does NOT cause air pollution?

(A) Increasing forest reserves
(B) Using pesticides in farms
(C) Developing housing estates
(D) Quarrying for limestone

Key

1	2	3	4	5	6	7	8	9	10	11	12	13	14	15	16	17	18	19	20
D	B	B	A	C	D	B	A	D	C	A	A	B	C	B	D	C	C	C	B

21	22	23	24	25
C	A	A	A	A

Food Production and Management

Synopsis

◆ **Agriculture** is the science or practice of growing crops.

◆ Plants of the same kind are grown and cultivated at one place on a large scale are called **crops**.

◆ There are three main crop seasons -

   (i)   **kharif** (June-September), **e.g.,** rice, jute, maize, groundnut and cotton.

   (ii) **rabi** (October-March), **e.g.,** wheat, mustard, potato, barley and gram.

   (iii) **summer crops**.

◆ **The steps involved** in cultivating a crop are as follows.

   ● Ploughing, levelling and manuring the soil.

   ● Sowing seeds at the correct depth and with right spaces between them. Some seeds are sown in nurseries and the seedlings are then transplanted to the main field.

   ● Improving soil fertility by adding manure and chemical fertilizers and also by adopting methods like crop rotation and leaving the field fallow.

   ● Ensuring irrigation at the right time.

   ● Protecting crops from weeds, pests and diseases either by using chemicals or by using natural methods.

   ● Harvesting, threshing and winnowing.

◆ Legumes are often used in crop rotation, because the nitrogen fixing bacteria which live in their roots improve soil fertility.

◆ Nitrogen fixation is a part of the nitrogen cycle, which is, continued cycling of nitrogen from the air to the soil and to living organisms.

◆ Grains are stored in silos or godowns that have been fumigated. Buffer stock is maintained for emergencies.

◆ Scientists have developed hybridisation processes to grow disease resistant varieties of plants. The earliest success is the production of high–yielding varieties of plants which led to increase in the production of food crops. This is often referred to as the **Green Revolution**.

◆ The branch of agriculture dealing with the rearing of farm animals is called **animal husbandry**.

◆ Animals give us milk, meat and eggs. Animal products are an excellent source of protein. Animal proteins are superior to plant proteins. Egg white contains the protein albumen.

Multiple Choice Questions

A B C D

1. Identify the term that is used to describe the science or practice of growing crops and covers all the activities of animals and cultivation.

(A) Animal husbandry
(B) Horticulture
(C) Agriculture
(D) Nurseries

2. Which of the following words would complete the given sequence?

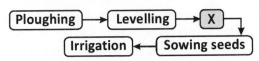

(A) Broadcasting (B) Transplanting
(C) Manuring (D) Drilling

3. Which of the following are the uses of machinery in agriculture ?

(A) Increase the quantity of crop yield.
(B) Get the job done faster.
(C) Reduce the dependency on human and animal labour.
(D) Both (B) and (C)

4. Which of the following processes involves transferring and combination of desirable characteristic features into plants and multiply them ?

(A) Eugenics
(B) Plant breeding
(C) Genetic engineering
(D) Crop improvement

5. Which of these is the correct sequence of steps to develop a new plant variety?

P – Evaluation
Q – Multiplication of improved seeds
R – Selection
S – Distribution of improved seeds
T – Development of gene variation

(A) T, R, P, Q, S   (B) R, T, P, Q, S
(C) S, Q, P, R, T   (D) P, Q, R, T, S

6. Which of the following helps in improving the quantity of food production?

(A) Pesticides.
(B) Synthetic hormones.
(C) Education and guidance to consumers.
(D) Optimum use of land for agriculture.

7. Which of these parts has nitrogen fixing bacteria in legumes?

(A) Leaves   (B) Flowers
(C) Root nodules (D) Stems

8. Which of the following are examples of an integrated cultivation system ?

(A) Breeding livestock on oil palm plantations
(B) Breeding small fishes in paddy fields
(C) Planting many types of crops on a small area
(D) Both (A) and (B)

9. Which of the following factors are utilised to increase food production and to meet the demand of an increasing population?

(A) Practicing efficient land management and development.
(B) Continuous research to ensure sustainable development.
(C) Using more pesticides to control pests.
(D) Both (A) and (B)

10. Which of the following are considered as modern technology in agriculture ?

(A) Genetic engineering is used to produce high quality traits in livestock and poultry
(B) Application of synthetic chemicals to improve soil fertility
(C) Using agromachinery for planting, harvesting and collecting agriculture produce
(D) All the above

11. Which methods of cultivation will result in the loss of soil fertility ?

(A) Crop rotation
(B) Shifting cultivation
(C) Excessive use of chemical fertilizers
(D) Both (B) and (C)

12. Which of the following is NOT a rabi crop?

(A) Rice   (B) Wheat
(C) Mustard   (D) Potato

13. Which of the following methods of cultivation causes salinisation of soil ?

(A) Transplantation
(B) Crop rotation
(C) Excessive irrigation
(D) Broadcasting

14. Which of the following classes of microorganisms play(s) an important role in the nitrogen cycle ?

(A) Bacteria   (B) Algae
(C) Fungi   (D) Both (A) and (B)

15. Which of the following information is/are true about nitrogen cycle ?

(A) Maintains the concentration of nitrogen in the air.
(B) Ensures a continuous source of protein.
(C) Increases water pollution.
(D) Both (A) and (B)

16. Which of the following terms is best suitable for stocking grains for emergencies ?

(A) Surplus stock (B) Storage
(C) Buffer stock   (D) Regular stock

17. Which of the following advantages do we get by using sprinkler system of irrigation?

(A) Helps the fields fill up wtih water
(B) Controls water supply
(C) Increases the evaporation of water
(D) Decrease the fertility of soil

18. Which of the following crops requires more irrigation ?

(A) Pulses   (B) Rice
(C) Maize   (D) Jowar

19. Which of the following shows the correct order of the given agricultural practices used during cultivation ?

(A) Ploughing, sowing, levelling, harvesting, manuring and irrigation
(B) Ploughing, levelling, irrigation, sowing, manuring and harvesting
(C) Ploughing, irrigation, sowing, manuring, harvesting and levelling
(D) Ploughing, levelling, manuring, sowing, irrigation and harvesting

20. Which of the following describes the advantage of ploughing ?

(A) It allows the penetration of roots of plants.
(B) It helps in proper aeration and eradicates weeds.
(C) It promotes the growth of useful soil bacteria.
(D) All of the above.

21. Which of the following practices does NOT improve the fertility of soil ?

(A) Keeping the land fallow
(B) Practising crop rotation
(C) Practising monocropping
(D) Practising multiple cropping

22. Which of the following agricultural practices keeps the fields free for a season to replenish the lost nutrients?

(A) Monocropping
(B) Crop rotation
(C) Multiple cropping
(D) Field fallow

23. In which of the following processes involves the removal of chaff from grain?

(A) Weeding   (B) Threshing
(C) Harvesting   (D) Winnowing

24. In which of the following agricultural methods does the farmer sows beans in his fields after harvesting a crop of wheat?

(A) Crop rotation
(B) Multiple cropping
(C) Fallow field
(D) Mixed cropping

25 Which of the following crops would enrich the soil with nitrogen ?

(A) Apple   (B) Pea
(C) Paddy   (D) Potato

26 Which of the following statements is NOT true ?

(A) The rotation of crops improves the fertility of soil.
(B) The rotation of crops saves a lot of nitrogenous fertilisers.
(C) The rotation of crops helps in weed and pest control.
(D) The rotation of crops helps in the maintenance of nutrients in the soil.

27 Which of the following methods enables us to select better and healthy seedlings for cultivation of rice ?

(A) Transplantation
(B) Broadcasting
(C) Chemical fertilisers
(D) All of the above

28 Which of the following is NOT true for chemical fertilizers ?

(A) They are nutrient specific.
(B) They are readily soluble in water.
(C) They provide humus to the soil.
(D) The overuse of chemical fertilisers pollutes the soil.

29 Which of the following options explain the term eutrophication ?

(A) Toxication of water by fertilisers
(B) Decrease the growth of algae
(C) Increase in the fertility of the soil
(D) All of the above.

30 Which of the following crops get attacked by Gundhi bug ?

(A) Wheat   (B) Sorghum
(C) Paddy   (D) Cotton

31 Which of the following disadvantages is / are caused due to the farming of high yielding varieties of crops ?

(A) They give less fodder.
(B) They require frequent weeding.
(C) They require higher inputs.
(D) All of the above.

32 Which of the following is the ill effect of green revolution ?

(A) Improvement in the economic condition of farmers
(B) Development of agriculture as an industry.
(C) Dependence on fertilisers, weedicides and pesticides.
(D) The wiping out of hunger and starvation.

33 Which of the following are the uses of animal husbandry ?

(A) Increase in milk production
(B) Proper utilisation of animal wastes
(C) Protection of animals against diseases
(D) All of the above

34 Which of the following programmes is also called operation flood ?

(A) Green revolution
(B) White revolution
(C) Black revolution
(D) Yellow revolution

35 Which of the following has been used for increasing productivity of super milk cows?

(A) Artificial insemination by only a pedigree bull.
(B) Super ovulation of only a high production cow only.
(C) Only embryo transplantation.
(D) A combination of all the above involving a carrier cow.

36 Which of the following is used as roughage in animals husbandry?

(A) Napier grass   (B) Cotton seeds
(C) Oil cakes   (D) Rice polish

37 Match the following correctly.

	Column - I		Column - II
a.	Kharif crops	(i)	Wheat
b.	Rabi crops	(ii)	Ploughing
c.	Tilling	(iii)	Harvesting
d.	Combine	(iv)	Paddy

(A) a-i, b-ii, c-iii, d-iv (B) a-iv, b-i, c-ii, d-iii
(C) a-iv, b-iii, c-ii, d-i (D) a-iii, b-iv, c-i, d-ii

38 Which of the following agricultural tools is used to level the field ?

(A) Harrow   (B) Leveller
(C) Seed drill   (D) Plough

39 Which of the following are removed by a harrow ?

(A) Weeds   (B) Crop plants
(C) Stones   (D) Rocks

40 Which of the following is an advantage of ploughing ?

(A) The loosening of soil.
(B) The distribution of nutrients.
(C) The removal of microorganisms.
(D) The removal of pests.

Previous Contest Questions

1 Which of the following weeds grows along with every crop ?

(A) Chenopodium
(B) Amaranthus
(C) Convolvulus
(D) Wild oat

2 Which of these agricultural implements is used to sow seeds ?

(A) Wooden plank (B) Seed driller
(C) Leveller   (D) Plough

3 Which of the following is made to prevent seed-borne diseases ?

(A) Sowing at the right depth
(B) Spacing at right intervals
(C) Sowing in highly wet soil
(D) Treat with fungicide solutions

4 Which of these elements is /are required to synthesise proteins ?

(A) Magnesium
(B) Nitrogen
(C) Potassium
(D) All of these

5 Which of these is fixed in root nodules of legumes by rhizobium bacteria?

(A) Magnesium   (B) Nitrogen
(C) Chlorine   (D) Manganese

6 Which of the following agricultural practices keeps the fields free for a season to replenish the lost nutrients ?

(A) Monocropping
(B) Crop rotation
(C) Multiple cropping
(D) Field fallow

7 Some farmers add a type of algae to barren field to support crop growth. Which algae did they use?

(A) Blue algae
(B) Green algae
(C) Blue green algae
(D) Brown algae

8 Which of the following is the correct sequence in farming ?

(A) Sowing → tilling → irrigation → manuring.
(B) Sowing → tilling → manuring → irrigation   .
(C) Levelling → manuring → sowing → irrigation.
(D) Sowing → tilling → manuring → irrigation.

9 Which of the following processes is also called field fallow ?

(A) Ploughing
(B) Irrigating
(C) Sowing
(D) Leaving the field uncultivated

10 Which of the following is a 'rabi' crop?

(A) Groundnut   (B) Maize
(C) Wheat   (D) Sugarcane

Cell

Synopsis

- The structural and functional unit of living organisms is a **cell**. Organisms that consist of only one cell are called **unicellular**. A tissue is made of cells. Tissues organise to form organs which in turn form organ systems and the organism.

- Cells without well organised nucleus, i.e., lacking nuclear membrane, are called **prokaryotic cells** and cells with definite nucleus are called **eukaryotic cells**.

- The cell is enclosed by a cell membrane enclosing the cytoplasm, nucleus and cell organelles.

- The cell membrane is selectively permeable, i.e., it lets the passage of certain substances only.

- The **cytoplasm** contains organelles, water and many dissolved substances such as proteins, carbohydrates, inorganic substances, fats, etc.

- The **nucleus** is bound by the nuclear membrane. Inside it, the nucleoplasm and a dense network of chromatin are present. Chromatin condenses during cell division and separates into chromosomes which bear genes.

- **Mitochondria** are the power houses of the cell. They use oxygen to oxidise food and release energy.

- **Endoplasmic reticulum** helps in the transport of substances within the cell. It is a network of tubelike structures.

- **Golgi body** is a stack of tubes and vesicles. It helps in the synthesis and storage of many substances. Some vesicles form lysosomes that digest and destroy cells. Hence they are called suicidal bags.

- **Centrioles** are present in animal cells. These help in the formation of astral fibres during cell division.

- **Plastids** are exclusively present in plants. They are of three types. **Chloroplasts** are photosynthetic in function. **Leucoplasts** are for storage and **chromoplasts** are coloured.

- **Vacuoles** are present in plant cells. It is covered by a tonoplast and has a vacuolar sap which stores food, wastes and water.

- Plant cells have a cell wall. It is thick, rigid and is made of **cellulose**. It gives support, shape and protection to the cell.

- The outermost region of the stem of a plant is called the **epidermis**. Ground tissue occupies most of the inner region. It consists of different types of tissues. The central core is called the **pith**, while the region inside the epidermis and extending up to the vascular bundles is called the **cortex**.

- The **vascular bundles** are distinct groups of cells arranged in a ring inside the stem. They consist of **xylem** and **phloem tissues**. Xylem cells transport water and minerals, while phloem cells transport food.

- There are four types of animal tissues **epithelial, muscular, connective** and **nervous**. Epithelial tissue is protective. Connective tissue has cells embedded in a matrix. Muscular tissue helps in movement. Nervous tissue consists of nerve cells. It makes up the brain and spinal cord.

Multiple Choice Questions   (A) (B) (C) (D)

1. Which of the following is the longest cell in human body ?

    (A) Nerve cells   (B) Muscle cells
    (C) Bone cells   (D) Gland cells

2. Which of the following tissues include blood cell ?

    (A) Epithelial tissue
    (B) Muscle tissue
    (C) Connective tissue
    (D) Nervous tissue

3. Which of the following is absent in an animal cell ?

    (A) Cytoplasm
    (B) Nucleus
    (C) Cell membrane
    (D) Cell wall

4. Which of the following is/are examples of an organ that contains a smooth muscle?

    (A) The Iris of eye (B) Uterus only
    (C) Bronchi only (D) All of these

5. Which of the following components is/are present in the nervous system ?

    (A) Brain
    (B) Spinal cord
    (C) Cranial and spinal nerves
    (D) All of these

6. Which type of tissues support, defend and store food in animals?

    (A) Epithelial   (B) Connective
    (C) Nervous   (D) Muscular

7. Which type of tissue lines our body cavities and covers body surface?

    (A) Nervous tissue
    (B) Muscle tissue
    (C) Epithelial tissue
    (D) Connective tissue

8. Which type of tissue is responsible for receiving, interpreting and producing a response to stimuli?

    (A) Muscle tissue
    (B) Nervous tissue
    (C) Epithelial tissue
    (D) Connective tissue

9. Which of the following statements is/are the functions of golgi apparatus ?

    (A) Transporting proteins that are to be released from the cell
    (B) Packaging proteins into vesicles.
    (C) Altering or modifying proteins.
    (D) All of these.

10. Which of the following is a saclike structure that store food, wastes and water ?

    (A) Lysosomes   (B) Centrosomes
    (C) Chromosomes (D) Vacuoles

11. Which of the following functions is performed by the carbohydrates of the plasma membrane ?

    (A) Passive transport
    (B) Active transport
    (C) Cell adhesion
    (D) Cellular recognition

12. Which of the following statements is the correct definition of a cell ?

    (A) The cell is the smallest part of a living being.
    (B) The cell is the part that can be seen only under a microscope.
    (C) The cell is the starting point in the life of all organisms.
    (D) The cell is the structural and functional unit of life.

13. Which of the following gives the cell its shape, maintains its size, protects the internal structures inside and is selectively permeable ?

    (A) Cell wall
    (B) Nuclear membrane
    (C) Cell membrane
    (D) Tonoplast

14. Which of the following is the jellylike substance inside the plasma membrane in which all the cell organelles are found floating ?

(A) Tonoplasm   (B) Cytoplasm
(C) Karyoplasm   (D) Cellsap

15. Which of the following is the largest organelle in the cell ?

(A) Nucleus   (B) Mitochondria
(C) Golgi complex (D) Lysosomes

16. Which of the following are the dense threadlike and rodlike structures present in the nucleus ?

(A) Golgi complex and chromatin.
(B) Chromosomes and Endoplasmic reticulum
(C) Centrosome and chromatin
(D) Chromatin and chromosome

17. Which of the following given below is in the ascending order of the number of nuclei present in cells?

(A) Paramoecium, brain cell, RBC of mammals.
(B) RBC of mammals, brain cell, paramoecium.
(C) Brain cell, RBC of mammals, paramoecium.
(D) All of these

18. Which of the following is the control room of the cell ?

(A) Nucleus   (B) Protoplasm
(C) Chloroplast   (D) Ribosome

19. Which of the following is the small rod shaped structure bound by a double membrane which helps in the oxidation of food to release energy ?

(A) Mitochondrion
(B) Golgi complex
(C) Nucleus
(D) Vacuole

20. Which of the following is called the energy currency of the cell ?

(A) MTP   (B) FTP
(C) ATP   (D) All of these

21. Which of the following is the intracellular transport structure that helps in the protein and lipid synthesis ?

(A) Ribosomes
(B) Microtubules and microfilaments
(C) Golgi complex
(D) Endoplasmic reticulum

22. Which of the following saclike structures help in the synthesis and storage of many substances?

(A) Endoplasmic reticulum
(B) Nucleus
(C) Mitochondria
(D) Golgi bodies

23. Which of the following organelles act as the digestive system within the cell?

(A) Golgi bodies   (B) Centrosomes
(C) Lysosomes   (D) Mitochondria

24. Which of the following cell organelles are respectively called suicidal bags and power houses of the cell ?

(A) Mitochondria and lysosomes.
(B) Lysosomes and mitochondria.
(C) Lysosomes and Golgi complex.
(D) Golgi complex and lysosomes.

25. Which of the following structures regulate cell division in animal cells?

(A) Chromosomes
(B) Chromatin
(C) Centrosome
(D) Spindle fibrils

26. Which of the following is true of the colourless plastid and its function?

(A) Chloroplasts performs photosynthesis
(B) Leucoplasts performs respiration
(C) Chromoplasts are involved with protection from sunlight
(D) Leucoplasts help in the storage of food

27 Which of the following is/are the green plastids ?

(A) Carotenoids   (B) Xanthophyll
(C) Chloroplasts (D) All the above

28 Which of the following is/are made up of cellulose ?

(A) Cell membrane
(B) Plasma membrane
(C) Cell wall
(D) All of these

29 Cheek cells are made up of which of the following cells ?

(A) Bone cells   (B) Epithelial cells
(C) Nerve cells   (D) Brain cells

30 Which of the following is the non-living part of the plant cell ?

(A) Nucleus   (B) Cytoplasm
(C) Mitochondrion   (D) Cell wall

Previous Contest Questions

1 Which of the following organelles is responsible for mechanical support and enzyme transport?

(A) Mitochondria
(B) Endoplasmic reticulum
(C) Chloroplast
(D) Golicomplex

2 Which of the following cell organelles receives the substances synthesized and released by the ER, condenses, modifies, packs and releases them in the form of secretory vesicles ?

(A) Golgi complex (B) Mitochondrion
(C) Lysosome   (D) Ribosome

3 Which of the following cell organelles does NOT contain DNA ?

(A) Mitochondria (B) Chloroplast
(C) Nucleus   (D) Lysosome

4 Which of these cellorganelles and their functions is matched correctly?

(A) Chloroplast – Controls all activities
(B) Nucleus – Gives shape to the body
(C) Cell wall – Synthesise food
(D) Mitochondria – Provides energy

5 Which of the following contain more mitochondria ?

(A) Germinating seeds
(B) Dry seeds
(C) Dormant seeds
(D) Soaked seeds

6 Which one of the following is a liquid connective tissue?

(A) Bone   (B) Blood
(C) Pancreas   (D) Liver

7 Which of the following is the correct combination ?

(A) Lysosomes – Intracellular digestion
(B) Microtubules – Respiration
(C) Mitochondria – Cell secretion
(D) Golgi complex – Energy

8 Which of the following tissues is/are present in stomach ?

(A) Muscle tissue
(B) Epithelial tissues
(C) Connective tissues
(D) All of these

9 Which of the following cells are long cells?

(A) Reproductive cells (B) Nerve cells
(C) Blood cells   (D) Cuboidal cells

10 Which of the following is the main difference between onion peel cells and human cheek cells ?

(A) Presence of mitochondria in onion peel cells
(B) Presence of cell wall in onion peel cells
(C) Absence of plasma membrane in cheek cells
(D) Absence of endoplasmic reticulum in cheek cells

CROSSWORD

1. Food Production and Management

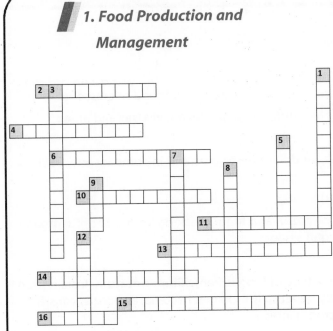

ACROSS

2 Animals kept in farms.
4 Crops grown in March/April.
6 The growing of leguminous crop in between two cereal or vegetable crops.
10 Gathering the produce on the maturity of a crop.
11 The rearing of honeybees.
13 Growing of two or more crops simultaneously.
14 Raising both, the plants crops and livestock in farm.
15 The science of raising and taking care of the domesticated animals, specially the livestock.
16 Crops like gram, pea, beans, pigeonpea, urd, moong, etc.

DOWN

1 The science of growing flowers, fruits and vegetables.
3 The planting of a crop in between two major crops.
5 Manure prepared from decayed animal and plant wastes.
7 Providing water to the crop at the right time.
8 Crops sown in the months of June/July.
9 Crops sown in the months of October/November.
12 Crops like paddy, wheat, maize, barley, oats etc.

2. Cell

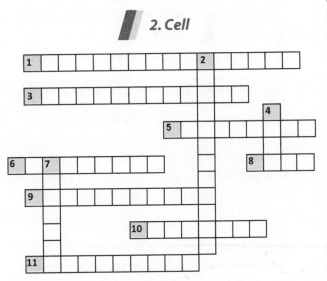

ACROSS

1 Organisms that lack nuclear membrane
3 Organisms made of more than one cell
5 The cell that receives and transfers messages
6 It is the jelly like substance present between the cell membrane and the nucleus
8 The basic structural unit of life
9 The organ that is used for locomotion in amoeba
10 Cell organelles that contain pigments
11 The largest cell

DOWN

2 Green coloured plastids
4 A unit of inheritance in living organisms
7 A group of similar cells performing a specific function

CHAPTER 3

Microorganisms

Synopsis

♦ **Microorganisms** are tiny organisms that can be seen only under a microscope.

♦ Microorganisms are classified into : **bacteria, fungi, protozoa, viruses** and **algae**.

Useful mocroorganisms:

♦ **E.coli** bacteria produce vitamins B_{12} and K. In herbivores and in some insects, bacteria and protozoa digest cellulose.

Decomposition and recycling of materials:

♦ Microorganisms such as bacteria, protozoa and fungi break down the harmful organic portion of raw sewage to less harmful sludge.

Medicine and health supplements :

♦ Antibiotic penicillin is produced by a type of fungus **Penicillium notatum**. Insulin used for treating diabetics is produced by genetically modified bacteria, a vaccine, consisting of dead or weakened harmful microorganisms.

Agriculture :

♦ Nitrogen fixation by **Rhizobium bacteria**, decomposition of organic wastes by saprophytic bacteria and fungi are some of the uses.

Industries :

♦ In food industry **lactic bacteria** is used in the preparation of curd and cheese. In making bread and in brewing alcoholic drinks, yeast is used.

Harmful Microorganisms :

Diseases caused by bacteria in humans.

Name of the disease	Name of the Pathogen	Symptoms of the disease
1. Cholera	Vibrio comma	Vomitings, loose motions
2. Leprosy	Mycobacterium leprae	Deformities of limbs
3. Gonorrhoea	Coccus bacteria	Pain in reproductive organs
4. Pneumonia	Diplococcus pneumoniae	Fluid in the lungs
5. Tetanus (lockjaw)	Clostridium tetani	Muscular spasms
6. Tuberculosis	Mycobacterium tuberculosis	Persistent cough, weight loss
7. Typhoid	Salmonella typhi	Fever

Diseases caused by bacteria in plants.

Blackrot in cabbage, fire blight in paddy

Diseases caused by Protozoans

Name of the disease	Name of the Pathogen	Symptoms of the disease
Dysentry	Entamoeba histolytica	Diarrhoea
Malaria	Plasmodium sps	High fever
Sleeping sickness	Trypanosoma gambiense	Fever

Diseases caused by virus.

Name of the disease	Symptoms of the disease
Common cold and influenza	Running nose, fever
Dengue fever	Running nose, fever, headache
Mumps	Fever, headache, swelling below the ear
Measles	Fever and red rashes
Poliomyelitis	Weak muscles, paralysis of the limbs
Rubella	Cough, fever
Chicken pox	Fever, headache, rashes
Acquired Immune Deficiency Syndrome (AIDS)	Intermittent fever, diarrhoea, loss of appetite, weight loss
Rabies	Hydrophobia attacks central nervous system

Diseases caused by virus in plants:

Corn stunt, little leaf of brinjal

Diseases caused by Fungi in animals.

Name of the disease	Symptoms of the disease
Ring worm	Scaly patches, itchy skin
Athlete's foot	Itchy rash between the toes

Diseases caused by fungi in plants:

Rust, smut, wilt and blight.

Multiple Choice Questions

(A) (B) (C) (D)

1 Which of the following is the smallest microorganism?

(A) Algae   (B) Bacterium
(C) Protozoan   (D) Virus

2 Identify W, X and Y?

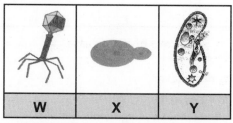

	W	X	Y

	(W)	(X)	(Y)
(A)	Virus	Protozoan	Fungus
(B)	Algae	Bacterium	Virus
(C)	Virus	Fungus	Protozoan
(D)	Fungus	Algae	Bacterium

3 Identify bacteriophage.

(A) Algae   (B) Virus
(C) Protozoa   (D) Fungi

4 Which of the following statements describes bacteriophage correctly?

(A) It is a bacterium which causes diseases in plants.
(B) It is a type of virus which attacks bacteria.
(C) It is a bacterium which kills viruses.
(D) It can multiply inside both living and non-living cells.

5 Fungi reproduces by

(A) Fission   (B) Fusion
(C) Seed formation (D) Spore formation

6 Which of the following characteristics places algae in the group of autotroph?

(A) Carrying out anaerobic respiration
(B) Manufacturing their own food
(C) Feeding on dead organisms
(D) Feeding on other living organisms

7 The moist bread becomes mouldy after a few days when it is left in a container with a cover. Which of the following conditions favour the growth of the fungus ?

(A) Absence of light
(B) Absence of water
(C) Presence of sunlight
(D) Presence of carbon dioxide

8 Which of the following microorganisms play an important role in maintaining the balance of nitrogen gas in the atmosphere?

(A) Viruses   (B) Bacteria
(C) Algae   (D) Protozoa

9 What causes the dough to rise when yeast is added to it?

(A) An increase in temperature
(B) An increase in the amount of substance
(C) An increase in the amount of released water by yeast cells
(D) The release of carbon dioxide gas

10 What process takes place when yeast is added to grape juice and left for a week?

(A) Decomposition (B) Fermentation
(C) Distillation   (D) Oxidation

11 Which of the following enzymes is secreted by bacteria that can digest cellulose ?

(A) Amylase   (B) Cellulase
(C) Lipase   (D) Protease

12 Which of the following is/are the functions performed by the microorganisms in the field of biotechnology ?

(A) The production of bioplastic
(B) The production of hormones
(C) Gene therapy
(D) Both (B) and (C)

13 Which of the following is/are produced by using bacteria ?

(A) Antibiotics   (B) Cheese
(C) Yoghurt   (D) All of these

14 Which of the following terms is given to the microorganisms that cause diseases?

(A) Antigens   (B) Antibodies
(C) Pathogens   (D) Vectors

15 Which of the following disease causing pathogens is / are carried by mosquitoes?

(A) Dengue fever
(B) Malaria
(C) Cholera
(D) Both (A) and (B)

16 Identify the disease that is caused by protozoa.

(A) Cholera   (B) Malaria
(C) Jaundice   (D) Hepatitis B

17 Which of the following options is/are true about the diseases, microorganisms which cause them and the symptoms of the diseases?

(A) Malaria, Protozoan, Fever and Chills
(B) Hepatitis B, Virus, Swollen liver
(C) Cholera, Virus, Vomiting, diarrhoea
(D) Both (A) and (B)

18 Which of the following can affectively prevent the ringworm disease ?

(A) Vaccination
(B) Vector control
(C) Improving personal hygiene
(D) Using antibiotics

19 Which of the following bacteria lives symbiotically in pea plants?

(A) Rhizobium   (B) Nitrosomonas
(C) Azotobacter   (D) Clostridium

20 Which of the following bacteria causes Cholera ?

(A) Streptococcus   (B) Clostridium
(C) Pasteurella   (D) Vibrio

21 Which of the following food components is digested by bacteria living in the intestines of herbivorous animals?

(A) Cellulose   (B) Proteins
(C) Fats   (D) Vitamins

22 Which of the following fungi have given one of the greatest drugs to the world of medicine ?

(A) Penicillium notatum
(B) Ustilago maydis
(C) Colletorichum falcatum
(D) Alternaria solani

23 Which one of the following is called pond silk?

(A) Spirogyra
(B) Volvox
(C) Chlamydomonas
(D) Euglena

24 Which of the following is the characteristic feature that distinguishes an algae from fungi?

(A) Heterotrophic   (B) Autotrophic
(C) Parasitic   (D) Sporophytic

25 How does Entamoeba histolytica enter the human body ?

(A) Through a mosquito bite
(B) Through Bird droppings
(C) Through Contaminated food and water
(D) Through a Sweat

26 Which of the following microorganisms causes common cold ?

(A) Bacteria   (B) Virus
(C) Protozoa   (D) Algae

27 Which of the following statements is true for viruses?

(A) Viruses multiply only in living host.
(B) Their crystals have a definite shape.
(C) Viruses grow and multiply by themselves outside the host.
(D) Viruses may be crystallized.

3. Microorganisms

28 How are microorganisms useful to us?

(A) The production of chemical fertilizers

(B) The production of fireworks

(C) The production of soft drinks

(D) The production of antibiotics

29 A microorganism X is used in the making of bread. It is also used in making which of the following substances ?

(A) Cheese   (B) Vinegar

(C) Wine   (D) Yoghurt

30 Through which of the following modes do most of the infectious diseases spread?

(A) Body contact (B) Air

(C) A vector   (D) All of these

Previous Contest Questions

1 Which of the following is represented by 'X' in the figure given below?

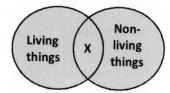

(A) Protozoa   (B) Bacteria

(C) Viruses   (D) Algae

2 Which of the following is the largest bacteria ?

(A) Bacillus   (B) Coccus

(C) Spirillum   (D) Spherical

3 Which of the following substances is/are produced by an organism to prevent or reduce the spread of microorganisms?

(A) Antiseptics   (B) Antibiotics

(C) Antibodies   (D) All of these

4 Which of the following organisms have an ability to help in recycling of nutrients and energy?

(A) Bacteria   (B) Diatoms

(C) Virus   (D) Fungi

5 What helps in diffentiating 'Spirogyra' from 'paramoecium'?

(A) Mitochondria (B) Golgi bodies

(C) Nucleus   (D) Plastids

6 Which of the following organisms can perform photosynthesis?

(A) Euglena   (B) Paramecium

(C) Mucor   (D) Mushroom

7 Which of the following microorganisms are used in making antibiotics?

(A) Viruses   (B) Fungi

(C) Bacteria   (D) Both (B) and (C)

8 Observe the given figure and identify P, Q, R and S.

P	Q
R	S

(A) P–Coccus, Q–Bacillus, R–Vibrio, S–Spirillum

(B) P–Bacillus, Q–Coccus, R–Spirillum, S–Vibrio

(C) P–Bacillus, Q–Vibrio, R–Coccus, S–Spirillum

(D) P–Bacillus, Q–Spirillum, R–Vibrio, S–Coccus

9 Which of the following pair is correct?

	Pathogens	Diseases caused
(A)	Viruses	Dengue fever
(B)	Bacteria	Malaria
(C)	Fungi	Hepatitis
(D)	Protozoa	Syphilis

10 Which of the following microorganisms exhibit symbiotic life?

(A) Lichens

(B) Volvox

(C) Blue green algae

(D) Spirogyra

3. Microorganisms

CHAPTER 4

Conservation of Plants and Animals

Synopsis

- The physical and biological world we live in is called **our environment**.

- **Biodiversity** refers to the variety of living organisms in a specific area.

- Plants and animals of a particular area are known as the **flora** and **fauna** of that area.

- The term **wildlife** refers to plants and animals living in the natural conditions. It serves as a source of genes or a gene bank.

- Over-exploitation of wildlife for economically useful products, deforestation, industrialisation and pollution resulted in extinction of several plant and animal species.

- **Red Data Book** contains a record of endangered species.

- **Conservation** involves keeping the natural environment in its balanced state as far as possible.

- **Preservation** involves keeping some of the earth's resources for future generations.

- The conservation of wildlife is linked with the conservation of forests and wetlands. India has 13 biosphere reserves, 92 national parks and 500 wildlife sanctuaries to help conserve wildlife.

- We should save, reuse and recycle paper to save trees, energy and water.

- In the whole universe earth is the only planet where life exists. It is our duty to make sure it remains beautiful, varied and a worthwhile place to live in.

- Natural disasters and human activities result in degeneration of biodiversity.

- There are endangered species exposed to danger of extinction. Endemic species are more endangered. They need conservation.

- Government at National and at State levels is taking all the care to conserve biodiversity.

- Forests must be preserved for biodiversity conservation.

- There are nearly 10 million of species of organisms on earth of which only 2 million have been identified and listed.

Multiple Choice Questions   (A) (B) (C) (D)

1 What is the variety of life and the diversity of genes, species and ecosystems of a region and their inter connectedness called?

(A) Biosphere
(B) Biodiversity
(C) Bioconservation
(D) Biocommunity

2 Which of the following is/are caused due to uncontrolled deforestation ?

(A) The destruction of habitats

(B) Landslides

(C) Floods

(D) All of these

3 Which of the following is the result of drought?

(A) Flooding
(B) Volcanic eruptions
(C) Decreased production of food
(D) Increased photosynthesis in plants

4 Which of the following includes all living organisms and all life-supporting regions of the Earth ?

(A) Biosphere   (B) Ionosphere
(C) Stratosphere (D) Lithosphere

5 Which of the following shows a modern technology measure that helps preserve and conserve the environment ?

(A) The practising crop rotation

(B) The recycling of paper, plastics and metal cans

(C) Using machines in agricultural industry

(D) Converting industrial wastes into biogas

6 Which of the following is an abiotic component ?

(A) Cow   (B) Grass
(C) Temperature (D) Bacteria

7 Which of the following are the effects of the mismanagement of timber logging?

(A) Floods   (B) Soil erosion
(C) Aforestation (D) Both (A) and (B)

8 Which of the following must be practised to preserve and conserve the environment?

(A) Deforestation (B) Recycling
(C) Soil erosion   (D) Pollution

9 Which of the following is the result of the introduction of exotic species?

(A) Conservation of wildlife.

(B) Maintenance of biodiversity.

(C) Adverse affect on native species adversely.

(D) The survival of native species.

10 Which of the following is/are advantage(s) of forests?

(A) Forests provide us with oxygen.

(B) They protect soil and provide habitat to a large number of animals.

(C) They help in bringing good rainfall in neighbouring areas .

(D) All of these

11 In which of the following practices a part of a forest cleared for cuttivation once before moving on to another new part?

(A) Shifting cultivation (B) Crop rotation
(C) Step farming   (D) All of these

12 Which of the following are the uses of IUCN Red List ?

(A) Developing awareness about the importance of threatened biodiversity

(B) Identification and documentation of endangered species

(C) Providing a global index of the decline of biodiversity

(D) All of these

13 Which of these animal projects protect endangered species?

(A) Tiger   (B) Elephant
(C) Crocodile   (D) All of these

14. What prevents soil erosion?

(A) Allowing herbivorous animals to graze excessively

(B) Growing plants to form the soil cover

(C) Increasing fertility

(D) Making the land sloppy

15. Which of the following is caused by deforestation ?

(A) Rainfall   (B) Soil erosion
(C) Weed control (D) Dim sunlight

16. What is the main aim of conserving living organisms?

(A) To increase the world's population of organisms

(B) To prevent the extinction of endangered species

(C) To help the students of botany and zoology

(D) To help in ecotourism

17. Which of the following are living resources in nature?

(A) Flora   (B) Fauna
(C) Soil   (D) Both (A) and (B)

18. What is an endangered animal?

(A) An animal on the verge of extinction

(B) An animal which is extinct

(C) An animal that is dangerous to humans

(D) An animal that is dangerous to other animals

19. Which of the following is/are factors that pose a great threat to biodiversity?

(A) Habitat destruction

(B) Disturbance and introduction of alien species

(C) Man's interference with nature

(D) All of these

20. Which of the following is the consequence of man's interference with nature?

(A) Increase in natural resources
(B) Biological imbalance
(C) Increase in the ozone layer
(D) Reappearance of extinct species

21. What is a National Park?

(A) An area strictly reserved for improvement of wild life

(B) An area where grazing and cultivation are permitted

(C) A park where the whole nation can have picnics

(D) A park which can be privately owned

22. Which of the following is the consequence of man's interference with nature?

(A) Afforestation
(B) Recycling of paper
(C) Poaching endangered animals
(D) Rain harvesting

23. What are species which are on the verge of extinction called?

(A) Endangered species
(B) Rare species
(C) Vulnerable species
(D) Fossil species

24. Which of the following is the biodiversity hot spot ?

(A) Oceans   (B) Rivers
(C) Deserts   (D) Forests

25. What is the direction in which energy flow in an ecosystem?

(A) Multidirectional (B) Unidirectional
(C) Bidirectional (D) Circular

26. Which of the following control methods can restore balance in an ecosystem?

(A) Rain water harvesting for conservation and management of water

(B) Conservation of ocean resources and preservation of marine life

(C) Public awareness programmes concerning conservation of wild life

(D) All of these

4. Conservation of Plants and Animals

27. Which of the following steps is NOT suitable for the conservation of tigers ?

    (A) Setting up sanctuaries to protect animals
    (B) Establishing forest reserves
    (C) Establishing more recreational and tourist centres in the forest
    (D) Increasing public awareness on the effects of indiscriminate hunting of animals

28. Which of the following is NOT a reason for the fall in biodiversity ?

    (A) Deforestation
    (B) Green revolution
    (C) Hunting
    (D) Environmental pollution

29. Which of the following methods of conservation helps in the maintaining of bio diversity?

    (A) Pollution   (B) Water sources
    (C) Gene pool   (D) Forest reserves

30. Which of the following is NOT true regarding the importance of wild life ?

    (A) Ecological value
    (B) Non-commercial value
    (C) Scientific value
    (D) Aesthetic value

31. Which of the following is NOT on the verge of extinction?

    (A) Leopard   (B) Nilgiri langur
    (C) The sloth   (D) Fox

32. Which of the following includes wildlife?

    (A) All non-domesticated and non-cultivated biota in their natural habitat
    (B) All domesticated and non-domesticated animals
    (C) All cultivated plants and non-domesticated animals
    (D) All non-cultivated plants and domesticated animals

33. Which of the following regions has rich flora and fauna ?

    (A) Deccan plateau (B) Lofty Himalayas
    (C) Himalaya slopes (D) Thar desert

34. In which of the following years Wildlife Protection act was passed ?

    (A) 1972   (B) 1970
    (C) 1982   (D) 1990

35. Which of the following is NOT an effective way to save living organisms from extinction?

    (A) Taking up afforestation
    (B) Establishing national parks
    (C) Importing organisms from other countries
    (D) Establishing centres to look after endangered species

Previous Contest Questions

1. Which of the following human activities may cause the extinction of species?

    (A) Using animal parts as traditional medicines
    (B) Encouraging game hunting as a sport
    (C) Using animal parts as decorative piece
    (D) All of these

2. Which of the following terms is used to describe the species of plants and animals that are found exclusively in a particular area called?

    (A) Endemic species
    (B) Endangered species
    (C) Rare species
    (D) Extinct species

3. Which of the following is caused by deforestation ?

    (A) Acid rain
    (B) Greenhouse effect
    (C) Increased oxygen content in the atmosphere
    (D) Decreased carbon dioxide content in the atmosphere

4. Which of the following is/are true of conservation and preservation?

(i) **Protects the ecosystem from destruction**
(ii) **Prevents the depletion of natural resources**
(iii) **Maintains the population of endangered plant and animal species**

(A) Only (i) and (ii)
(B) Only (i) and (iii)
(C) Only (ii) and (iii)
(D) All the three

5. Name the State that launched 'Project elephant' to save Asian elephants?

(A) Tamilnadu
(B) Andhra Pradesh
(C) Maharashtra
(D) Karnataka

6. What should be done for species preservation?

(A) Protecting areas that have endangered species
(B) Protecting the breeding grounds of endangered species
(C) Issuing hunting licence to VIPs
(D) Both (A) and (B)

7. Under man and biosphere programme (MAB), what is a core zone?

(A) A zone where human activity is permitted
(B) A zone where human activity is not permitted
(C) A zone where controlled hunting is permitted
(D) A zone where slash and burn cultivation is permitted

8. Which of the following processes will help in the conservation of natural resources ?

(A) The maintaining of the earth's resources in their original state
(B) The using of earth's resources wisely
(C) The using of resources not in a wasteful manner
(D) Both (B) and (C)

9. Which of the following processes include the mass emigration of bees to settle down at a newplace in order to form a new hive called?

(A) Migration   (B) Swarming
(C) Spawning   (D) Carting

10. Why is the proper management of the environment important?

(A) Humans can continue to live.
(B) Animals would not become extinct.
(C) The balance nature can be preserved.
(D) All of the above.

CROSSWORD

3. Microorganisms

ACROSS

1   Microbes helping in fermentation of food

3   A substance obtained from a living organism which is poisonous for another living organism

4   Rod shaped bacteria

5   Single celled animals

9   Virus that attacks and lives on bacteria

11   Bacteria that fixes atmospheric nitrogen in the root nodules of legumes

12   Harmful microbes

13   Comma shaped bacteria

14   A single celled animal

DOWN

2   Malarial parasite

6   Disease causing germs

7   Germs of a disease used for cultivating antibodies in another living animals

8   Tiniest of all the known microbes

10   Disease causing germs

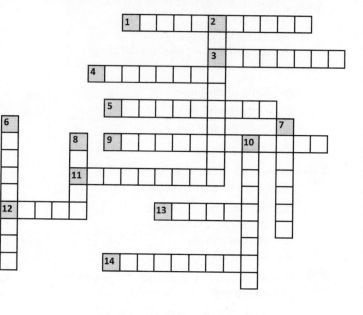

4. Conservation of Plants and Animals

ACROSS

2   The term that is used to name all types of animals

8   Scientific name of human beings

11   A flightless bird that has disappeared from Marutius

12   Species restricted to a region

13   Removal of forests to use the land for agriculture

DOWN

1   Animals at the verge of being endangered

3   Areas reserved for wildlife where they can freely use the habitats and natural resources

4   The total number of life forms on the Earth

5   Areas where animals are protected from danger to them and disturbance to their habitat

6   A group of individuals having structural and functional similarity

7   Human activity that leads to the loss of certain species to get economical benefit

9   Species towards extinction or disappearance

10   The group that includes all types of plants on this Earth.

CHAPTER 5

Reproduction in Animals

Synopsis

◆ **Reproduction** is the production of new individuals more or less similar to the parent organisms. This may be achieved by a number of means and serves to perpetuate increase of species.

◆ There are two main methods in which organisms give rise to new individuals - **Asexual reproduction** and **sexual reproduction**.

◆ **Asexual reproduction** is the process of producing new organism(s) from a single parent without the involvement of sex cells or gametes.

e.g., Binary fission in amoeba, regeneration in planaria, budding in hydra.

◆ **Sexual reproduction** is the process of producing new organism(s) from two parents with the involvement of sex cells or gametes. Male sexual unit is known as male gamete or sperm while female sexual unit is termed as female gamete or ova.

◆ The fusion of sperm and ovum is known as **fertilisation**. Thus, the two major processes, i.e., formation of gametes and fusion of gametes constitute sexual reproduction.

◆ The reproductive organs of human beings, i.e., testes is in male and ovaries in female produce gametes and also secrete hormones like testosterone (male hormone), estrogen and progesterone (female hormones).

◆ Fertilisation takes place in the fallopian tube. The embryo develops in the uterus, and receives oxygen and nutrients through the placenta.

◆ Animals such as human beings, cows, dogs which give birth to young ones are called **viviparous animals**. Animals such as hen, frog, lizard which lay eggs are oviparous animals.

◆ The transformation from the larval stage to the adult stage in the life cycles of frog and insects is called **metamorphosis**.

◆ The **cloning of animals** produces offspring with genetic materials which are identical to the parent. The most famous animal clone is **Dolly**, the sheep.

Multiple Choice Questions   (A) (B) (C) (D)

1 Which of the following statements is true about asexual reproduction?

(A) New individuals are produced without the fusion of gametes.

(B) New individuals involves the fusion of male and female gametes.

(C) It is a mode of reproduction which occurs only in plants.

(D) New individuals are produced by the fusion of dissimilar gametes.

2 Which of the following is NOT a characteristic feature of sexual reproduction?

(A) It involves the fusion of two reproductive cells.

(B) It is common in most organisms.

(C) Fertilization may take place inside or outside the body of the female.

(D) The offspring receives its characteristics from one parent only.

3 Which of the following is NOT an example of asexual reproduction?

(A) Reproduction in hydra

(B) Reproduction in amoeba

(C) Reproduction in bacteria

(D) Reproduction in butterfly

4 Which of the following is/are paired structure in human reproductive system?

(A) Ovary   (B) Testes

(C) Fallopian tube (D) All of these

5 Which of the following statements about the human female egg cell is incorrect?

(A) It is produced when a female reaches puberty.

(B) The two ovaries in a female alternately produce the egg cells.

(C) One egg cell is usually produced by a female every 28 days.

(D) An egg cell can live in the body of a female for about a month.

6 Identify W, X, Y and Z in the given figure.

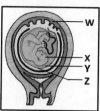

	(W)	(X)	(Y)	(Z)
(A)	Placenta	Foetus	Amniotic fluid	Foetal membrane
(B)	Umbilical cord	Embryo	Uterus	Vagina
(C)	Placenta	Foetus	Uterus	Foetal membrane
(D)	Umbilical cord	Zygote	Amniotic fluid	Cervix

7 Which part within the uterus prevents the mixing of the blood of the foetus with that of the mother ?

(A) Umbilical cord   (B) Uterus wall

(C) Placenta   (D) Water sac

8 Which of the following sequences is in the correct order?

(A) Zygote → Embryo → Foetus → Baby

(B) Zygote → Embryo → Baby → Foetus

(C) Embryo → Zygote → Baby → Foetus

(D) Foetus → Zygote → Embryo → Baby

9 Which of the following is NOT true of the process of reproduction?

(A) Unicellular organisms cannot reproduce.

(B) Reproduction is the process of producing young animals or plants.

(C) Reproduction is one of the life processes of living things.

(D) Reproduction is of two types, sexual and asexual reproduction.

10 Which of these organisms reproduce in the same way as yeast ?

(A) Hydra   (B) Amoeba
(C) Starfish   (D) Flatworm

11 Which of the following is/are types of asexual reproduction?

(A) Budding   (B) Binary fission
(C) Spore formation (D) All the above

12 Which of the following comparisons are true of sexual and asexual reproduction?

	Sexual reproduction	Asexual reproduction
(i)	Involves two individuals	Involves only one individual parent
(ii)	Involves a simple process	Involves a complex process
(iii)	Involves the union of two types of gametes	No fusion of gametes

(A) Only (i) and (ii) (B) Only (i) and (iii)
(C) Only (ii) and (iii) (D) All the above

13 How are Paramoecium and Amoeba are similar?

(A) Unicellular.
(B) Does not have a nucleus.
(C) Reproduces by binary fission.
(D) Both (A) and (C)

14 In which of the following parts of the female reproductive system does fertilisation occur ?

(A) Ovary   (B) Vagina
(C) Uterus   (D) Fallopian tube

15 Identify R, S and T in the given figure.

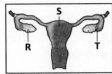

	(R)	(S)	(T)
(A)	Ovulation	Fertilization	Implantation
(B)	Fertilization	Ovulation	Implantation
(C)	Ovulation	Implantation	Fertilization
(D)	Implantation	Fertilization	Ovulation

16 Read the given information and identify P, Q and R.

P	–	An ovum is discharged by the ovary
Q	–	An embryo is implanted in the uterus
R	–	The fusion of male and female gametes takes place

	(P)	(Q)	(R)
(A)	Ovulation	Implantation	Fertilization
(B)	Fertilization	Implantation	Ovulation
(C)	Ovulation	Fertilization	Implantation
(D)	Implantation	Ovulation	Fertilization

17 What is the function of the amniotic fluid?

(A) It provides food to the foetus.
(B) It provides oxygen to the foetus.
(C) It protects the foetus from shock.
(D) It protects the foetus from diseases.

18 The substances that are transported through umbilical cord

(A) Urea.   (B) Antibodies.
(C) Carbon dioxide (D) All of these

19 Which of the following labelled stages grow within a case during development?

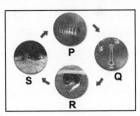

(A) P   (B) Q
(C) R   (D) S

20 In which of the following animals fertilisation is external?

(A) Birds and fish
(B) Amphibians and birds
(C) Reptiles and fish
(D) Fish and amphians

21 How many cells are formed as a result of binary fission ?

(A) 2 (B) 3 (C) 1 (D) 4

22 Which of the following is called the larva of a frog ?

(A) Nymph   (B) Tadpole
(C) Caterpillar (D) Fry

23 Which of the following processes refers to the casting away of the skin by a caterpillar to allow a larger caterpillar to emerge ?

(A) Metamorphosis (B) Chrysalis
(C) Moulting   (D) Development

24 Which of the following shows the correct route, that the sperm takes after leaving the testis ?

(A) Epididymis - vas deferens - ejaculatory duct - urethra.

(B) Vas deferens - epididymis - urethra - ejaculatory duct.

(C) Ejaculatory duct - epididymis - vas deferens - urethra.

(D) Epididymis - vas deferens - urethra - ejaculatory duct.

25 Which of the following structures has an internal wall lined with fingerlike projections ?

(A) Ovary   (B) Vagina
(C) Fallopian tube (D) Uterus

26 Which of the following organs contains seminiferous tubules ?

(A) Kidney   (B) Ovary
(C) Testes   (D) Brain

27 In which of the following organs sperms mature ?

(A) Testes   (B) Epididymis
(C) Vasdeferns (D) Cowper's glands

28 In which of the following processes is ovum released from the follicle ?

(A) Ovulation   (B) Oogenesis
(C) Capacitation (D) Menstrual cycle

29 Which of the following is an unpaired structure in the human reproductive system?

(A) Ovary   (B) Testes
(C) Fallopiantube (D) Uterus

30 Which of the following is correct of implantation ?

(A) Attachment of the blastocyst to the uterine wall

(B) Release of ovum from the follicle

(C) Development of an embryo without fertilisation

(D) Formation of ova from germ cells

31 Which of the following is a specialised structure that provides nourishment to the foetus from the mother and collects wastes from it, passing them onto the mother ?

(A) Fallopian tube   (B) Placenta
(C) Cowper's gland   (D) Blastocyst

32 Which of the following are found in high concentrations in the blood that passes from the placenta to the foetus ?

(A) Urea and carbon dioxide
(B) Urea and glucose
(C) Carbon dioxide and antibiotics
(D) Oxygen and amino acids

33 Which of the following is the function of substance that is secreted by cowper's gland?

(A) Protecting sperms
(B) Serving as a lubricant
(C) Turning the semen alkaline
(D) Helping the sperm in penetrating the ovum

34 Which of the following organisms reproduces asexually?

(A) Protozoa   (B) Frog
(C) Lizard   (D) Housefly

35 AIDS is a deadly disease which is caused by

(A) a protozoan. (B) a fungus.
(C) a bacterium. (D) a virus.

Previous Contest Questions

1 Which of the following organisms contains ampluxory pads that help in copulation ?

(A) Earthworm   (B) Frog
(C) Fish   (D) Butterfly

2 Which of the following is/are present in the milt of frog ?

(A) Embryo
(B) Ovum
(C) Spermatozoa
(D) Both (A) and (C)

3 Which of the following statements are correct about menstrual cycle?

(A) A girl who has reached puberty will menstruate throughout her life.
(B) Menstruation occurs every 28 days
(C) During every menstrual cycle, one mature ovum will be released by the ovary.
(D) Both (B) and (C)

4 Which part within the uterus prevents the mixing of the blood of the foetus with that of the mother ?

(A) Umbilical cord (B) Uterus wall
(C) Placenta   (D) Water sac

5 Which of the following is an oviparous mammal ?

(A) Echidna   (B) Kangaroo
(C) Rabbit   (D) Bat

6 Identify the process shown below.

(A) Fission   (B) Fertilisation
(C) Conjugation   (D) Ovulation

7 Which of the following terms is used to describe the mass of eggs of a frog ?

(A) Follicles   (B) Ostium
(C) Spawn   (D) Both (A) & (B)

8 In which of the following organisms does internal fertilization occurs?

(A) Bird and fish
(B) Snake and frog
(C) Rabbit and frog
(D) Snake and Rabbit

9 Which of the following organs contain graafian follicles ?

(A) Fallopian tube (B) Uterus
(C) Vagina   (D) Ovary

10 How many ova is/are released at a time in the female human being?

(A) 4   (B) 3
(C) 2   (D) 1

Reaching the Age of Adolescence

Synopsis

◆ Humans become capable of reproduction after puberty sets in. Between the ages of 11 years and 19 years children are called **adolescents**.

◆ The period of time when a person changes from a child into an adult is called **puberty**.

◆ A boy reaches puberty when he is 13-14 years old. Girls reach puberty earlier than boys at the age of 11-12 years.

◆ During puberty, physical and emotional changes take place. These are called secondary sexual characters. In girls, puberty is marked by the onset of menstruation and the development of secondary sexual characters, namely, enlargement of breasts, widening of pelvic girdle and growth of hair in the armpits and pubic region.

◆ In boys, puberty begins with the production of sperms and is marked by secondary sexual characters, namely, deepening of the voice, growth of hair on the face, armpits and pubic region and enlargement of the scrotum and penis.

◆ **Menstruation** is the periodic discharge of blood from the uterus through the vagina. The discharged blood usually contains a dead egg cell and some tissues from the lining of the uterus.

◆ If the egg cell is fertilized, it will form a zygote which will implant itself on the wall of the uterus. It will eventually develop into an embryo. Menstruation does not take place during pregnancy.

◆ The onset of puberty and maturity of reproductive parts are controlled by **hormones**.

◆ Hormones are secretions of endocrine glands which are poured directly into the blood stream.

◆ **Pituitary gland** secretes hormones which include growth hormone and hormones that make other glands such as those of the testes, ovaries, thyroids and adrenals secrete hormones. **Pancreas** secretes insulin, **thyroid** produces thyroxine and adrenals produce adrenaline.

◆ **Testosterone** is the male hormone and **estrogen** is the female hormone. The uterine wall in females prepares itself to receive the developing fertilised egg. In case there is no fertilisation, the thickened lining of the uterine wall breaks down and goes out of the body along with blood. This is called menstruation.

◆ The sex of the unborn child depends on whether the zygote has **XX** or **XY** chromosomes.

◆ It is important to eat balanced food and maintain personal hygiene during adolescence.

◆ **Personal hygiene** must be maintained during menstruation to avoid itch, unpleasant odour, bacterial and fungal infection.

Multiple Choice Questions   (A) (B) (C) (D)

1 Which of the following statements is true?

(A) Boys reach puberty at an earlier age than girls.

(B) Girls reach puberty earlier than boys.

(C) At the end of rapid growth, girls are normally heavier than boys.

(D) Between the age of 4 to 12, girls grow faster than boys.

Answer the questions from 2 to 5 based on the graph given below.

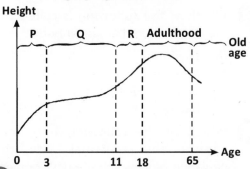

2 Which of the following represents growth periods labelled as P, Q and R ?

(A) P-Infancy, Q-Childhood, R-Old age

(B) P-Infancy, Q-Childhood, R-Adolescence

(C) P-Adulthood, T-Adolescence, R-Old age

(D) P-Childhood, Q-Infancy, R-Adolescence

3 When does adolescence occur?

(A) 0 to 3 years   (B) 3 to 13 years

(C) 11 to 18 years   (D) 18 to 45 years

4 What are the two different periods that show rapid growth rate ?

(A) Infancy and adolescence

(B) Adulthood and old age

(C) Infancy and childhood

(D) Adolescence and old age

5 During which of the following stages of growth in height is maximum?

(A) At the end of adulthood

(B) Before puberty

(C) At the beginning of old age

(D) At the beginning of adulthood

6 What is the role of sperms in reproduction ?

(A) To stimulate ovum

(B) To fertilize the egg

(C) To form foetus

(D) To initiate changes in male during puberty

7 What causes changes in females at the time of puberty?

(A) Sex cells   (B) Enzymes

(C) Nutrients   (D) Sex hormones

8 Which of the following will occur in females at puberty?

(A) Ovulation

(B) Enlargement of breasts

(C) Broadening of hips

(D) All of these

9 A girl has menstruation on the 6th day of the month. When is ovulation most likely to occur?

(A) 15th - 17th day (B) 18th - 20th day

(C) 23rd - 25th day (D) 27th - 28th day

10 When do girls overtake boys in height?

(A) Childhood   (B) Adolescence

(C) Adulthood   (D) Old age

11 In girls, secondary sexual characteristics develop between

(A) 9 and 11 years.   (B) 11 and 14 years.

(C) 15 and 18 years. (D) 19 and 21 years.

12 Why is a diet rich in proteins essential at puberty?

(A) For supplying sufficient energy

(B) For the formation of new cells during growth

(C) the formation of strong bones and teeth

(D) protection from diseases

13 Which of the following is NOT a secondary sexual characteristic feature of girls?

(A) The enlargement of breasts.

(B) The deepening of voice.

(C) The menstruation begins.

(D) The growth of hair at armpit.

14 Which of the following is/are true of secondary sexual characteristics of boys?

(A) Growth of facial hair
(B) Development of bones and muscles
(C) Production of sperms
(D) All of these

15 The menstrual cycle stops in a women at about 50 years old. The woman is said to have reached

(A) puberty.   (B) menopause.
(C) menarche.   (D) adolescence.

16 Which of the following does not take place during the final stage of the menstrual cycle?

(A) Further thickening of the uterine lining.
(B) Repair and growth of the uterine lining.
(C) Ovulation.
(D) Both (B) and (C)

17 Which of these hormones is secreted by endo- crine gland located on the top of kidneys?

(A) Adrenaline   (B) Insulin
(C) Progesterone (D) Testosterone

18 Which of the following pairs of hormones and minerals is associated with the occurrence of goitre?

	Minerals	Hormones
(A)	Iron	Insulin
(B)	Iodine	Thyroxine
(C)	Calcium	Thyroxine
(D)	Phosphorus	Adrenaline

19 Incomplete development of male secondary sexual characteristics is caused due to deficiency in?

(A) Estrogen.   (B) Progesterone.
(C) Adrenaline.   (D) Testosterone.

20 Which of the following hormones initiates metamorphosis in insects ?

(A) Thyroxine   (B) Insulin
(C) Growth hormone (D) Adrenaline

21 Which chromosomes determine the sex of an individual?

(A) Autosomes
(B) Allosomes
(C) Plasmid
(D) Giant chromosomes

22 What is the legal age for boys and girls to get married in our country ?

(A) 18 years for boys, 21 years for girls.
(B) 21 years for boys, 18 years for girls.
(C) 23 years for boys, 20 years for girls.
(D) 25 years for boys, 18 years for girls.

23 Which of the following is called the master gland in the human body ?

(A) Thyroid
(B) Adrenal
(C) Islets of langerhans
(D) Pituitary

24 Which of the following hormones controls the menstrual cycle, the ovulation process and the development of the uterus in the females ?

(A) Estrogen   (B) Progesterone
(C) Testosterone (D) Both (A) and (B)

25 Which of the following transports hormones from the place of origin to the place of target?

(A) Ducts   (B) Blood
(C) Nerves   (D) All of these

Previous Contest Questions

1 Arjun kept losing weight even though he was taking his meals regularly. He felt thirsty all the time. When the doctor tested Arjun's urine, the test showed a high concentration of glucose. What disease is Arjun suffering from?

(A) Goitre.
(B) Cancer.
(C) Diabetes mellitus.
(D) Cirrohsis of the liver.

2 Which of the following processes involves the fusion of a male and female gamete ?

(A) Fertilisation   (B) Fission
(C) Implantation   (D) Insemination

3 Which of the following factors determine the sex of the offspring in humans ?

(A) Mother's sex chromosomes
(B) Father's sex chromosomes
(C) Mother's vegetative chromosomes
(D) Father's vegetative chromosomes

4 Identify the correct sequence that is followed during the growth of human being?

1.	Foetus	2.	Zygote
3.	Embryo	4.	Baby
5.	Adult	6.	Adolescent
7.	Child		

(A) 2, 3, 1, 4, 7, 6, 5.   (B) 2, 1, 3, 4, 7, 5, 6.
(C) 3, 2, 1, 4, 6, 7, 5.   (D) 1, 3, 2, 4, 7, 6, 5.

5 The given table has various stages.

> W – The ovum dies within 24 hours after ovulation.
>
> X – The uterus wall thickens with blood vessels.
>
> Y – The uterus wall breaks down.
>
> Z – The ovary discharges an ovum.

Which of these sequence is correct of the menstrual cycle?

(A) W, Y, X, Z   (B) X, Z, W, Y
(C) Y, W, Z, X   (D) Z, X, Y, W

6 What do X, Y and Z represent in the figure given below ?

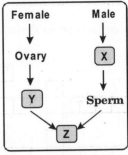

(A) X-Ovum, Y-testes, Z-Ovulation
(B) X-Testes, Y-Ovum, Z-Implantation
(C) X-Ovum, Y-Testes, Z-Implantation
(D) X-Testes, Y-Ovum, Z-Fertilization

7 Which of the following parts secretes testosterone ?

(A) Tunica albuginea
(B) Interstitial cells
(C) Germinal epithelium
(D) Sertoli cells of testes

8 Which of the following endocrine glands is nearest to the heart ?

(A) Thyroid   (B) Pancreas
(C) Thymus   (D) Adrenal

9 Which of the following represents the composition of female destined zygote in human beings ?

(A) 22 + X.   (B) 44 + XY.
(C) 33 + Y.   (D) 44 + XX.

10 Which of the following body fluids does not transmit HIV ?

(A) Blood   (B) Breast milk
(C) Tears   (D) Semen

CROSSWORD

5. Reproduction in Animals

ACROSS

1 The stage of the embryo in which all the body parts can be identified
4 The fusion of the egg and the sperm
7 The type of reproduction that involves the fusion of male and female gametes
8 A single cell that is formed as a result of the fusion of the egg cell and a sperm
10 Animals which lay eggs
12 The transformation of the larva into an adult through drastic changes
13 The process that is essential for the continuation of a species

DOWN

2 Female gametes
3 The animals which give birth to young ones
5 Reproduction in Hydra
6 Reproduction in Amoeba
9 Male gametes
11 A ball of cells that begin to form groups which then develop into tissues and organs

6. Reaching the Age of Adolescence

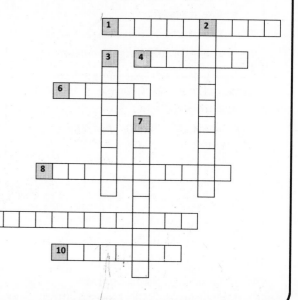

ACROSS

1. The period of life during which there are changes in the body leading to reproductive maturity
4 The period during which the body undergoes changes during adolescence.
6 The Voice box
8 The diet that is planned to provide sufficient nutrients required for the body
9 The gland that releases hormones and stimulates testes and ovaries to release testosterone and oestrogen
10 The chemical substance that controls changes that occur during adolescence

DOWN

2 Thread like structures that carry genes
3 The hormone that controls metamorphosis in frog
5 The voice box in boys that can be seen as a protruding part at the throat
7 The hormone that helps the body to adjust to stress

Model Test Paper

Score /25

1 Which of these are called weeds ?

(A) Microbes   (B) Unwanted plants
(C) Insects   (D) Fungal pest

2 The gland that plays a key role in the metamorphosis of frog's tadpole is

(A) thymus   (B) thyroid
(C) adrenal   (D) pancreas

3 Which of these statement is true about migration ?

(A) The phenomenon of restocking of destroyed biodiversity
(B) The movement of animals to get protection from preying animals.
(C) The phenomenon of movement of a species from its own habitat to some other habitat for a particular period.
(D) The phenomenon of changing body colour and patterns.

4 Which cell organelle is pigmented ?

(A) Mitochondria (B) Golgi bodies
(C) Nucleus   (D) Plastids

5 Which of these terms is associated with rearing fishes?

(A) Pisciculture   (B) Poultry
(C) Apiculture   (D) Sericulture

6 Which of the following is a protozoan disease?

(A) Tetanus
(B) Measles
(C) Filariasis
(D) Sleeping sickness

7 Which of the following indicates the stoppage of menstruation ?

(A) Meanarche   (B) Period
(C) Menopause   (D) Menstruation

8 Which of the following does not contain chloroplasts?

(A) Cycas   (B) Moss
(C) Mushroom   (D) Fern

9 A student waiting for his results feels nervous and the rate of his heartbeat increases. Which of these hormones causes this condition ?

(A) Insulin   (B) Oestrogen
(C) Adrenaline   (D) Thyroxine

10 Which of the following inventions will make the farmer's work easier?

(A) Threshers
(B) Harvesting machine
(C) Ploughs pulled by tractors
(D) Automatic irrigation system

11 Which of the following is observed on a slice of moist bread when left in a dark place for a few days ?

(A) Bread dries.
(B) Fungal mycelium is developed.
(C) Algae develops.
(D) Waterdrops accumulate.

12 In a biology class the teacher described a cell. She listed the following organelles. of the cell – endoplasmic reticulum, mitochondria, nucleus, ribosome, centriole and centrosome. Which cell was she referring to?

(A) Prokaryotic cell
(B) Plant cell
(C) Animal cell
(D) It is not possible to predict from the given data

13. What will be the genetic material found in a sperm?

(A) 22+X   (B) 22 + Y
(C) 23 + XY   (D) Both (A) and (B)

14. Which of the following reproduces in the same way as hydra ?

(A) Virus   (B) Yeast
(C) Bacterium (D) Protozoan

15. Which of the following cell organelles carries heriditary material ?

(A) Genes   (B) Protoplasm
(C) Cytoplasm (D) Plastid

16. Where does the fertilization of the female egg occurs in human beings ?

(A) Vagina   (B) Uterus
(C) Ovary   (D) Fallopian tube

17. Which of the following is/are vectors of malaria fever ?

(A) Culex   (B) Aedes
(C) Anopheles (D) All of the above

18. Sex hormones are responsible for all of the following in the female except for _____.

(A) the maturation of ova in the ovary
(B) the maturation of thinking
(C) the change of body shape
(D) menstruation

19. Which of the following is a storage organelle?

(A) Mitochondria (B) Leucoplast
(C) Chloroplast (D) Ribosome

20. Red data book contains list of

(A) endangered species of plant and animals.
(B) extinct animals and plants.
(C) exotic plants and birds.
(D) rare species of plants and animals.

21. Adrenal gland in mammals is located

(A) near pituitary (B) near liver
(C) near heart   (D) above kidney

22. Which of these is a multicellular algae?

(A) Volvox   (B) Chlamydomonas
(C) Spirogyra (D) Chlorella

23. Which of these is oviparous?

(A) Echidna   (B) Bat
(C) Cat   (D) Rat

24. Match the following plants in Column-I with their answers in Column-II.

Column - I	Column - II
(a) Maize	i. Inter crop
(b) Wheat	ii. Rabi crop
(c) Trifolium	iii. Kharif crop
(d) Blue-green algae	iv. Nitrogen fixing organism

(A) a -II, b-III, c-I, d-IV (B) a-I, b-II, c-III, d-IV
(C) a-III, b-II, c-I, d-IV (D) a-III, b-I, c-II, d-IV

25. The flow chart given below represents sexual reproduction.

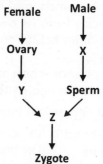

Which of the following represents X, Y and Z in the given figure?

	(X)	(Y)	(Z)
(A)	Ovum	Testes	Ovulation
(B)	Testes	Ovum	Implantation
(C)	Ovum	Testes	Implantation
(D)	Testes	Ovum	Fertilization

Key

1	2	3	4	5	6	7	8	9	10	11	12	13	14	15	16	17	18	19	20
B	B	C	D	A	D	C	C	C	B	B	C	D	B	A	D	C	B	B	A

21	22	23	24	25
D	C	A	C	D

Questions@stimulating-minds

1. A sealed tank has a capacity of 3000 cm^3. It is half-filled with water. An air syringe is attached to an opening as shown below.

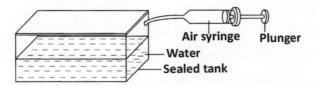

Each time the plunger is pushed in, 200 cm^3 of air is pumped into the tank. What will be the total volume of air inside the tank if the piston is pushed in thrice ?

2. What is the average surface area and air pressure acting on a human body ?

3. The larger the surface area of contact, the larger the frictional force. Is it true ?

4. What are the three ways by which a cyclist in a race can reduce air friction to the minimum?

5. How does an air-puck shown below moves smoothly on a table ?

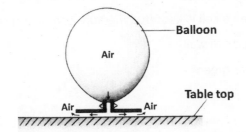

6. What is stereophonic hearing and how does it occur in our body ?

7. What gives rise to an optical illusion ? Explain with examples ?

8. What are the limitations of our sight ?

9. How are stars classified ?

10. Why the formation of a polymer like polyethene requires the presence of a catalyst?

11. Why are silver, gold and platinum made into jewellery, but iron is not?

12. From the series of reactive metals, aluminium would be expected to be very reactive and easily corrosible. Yet, it is hardly corroded by air or chemicals. Why?

13. What is the volume occupied by natural gas?

14. Water is the most common extinguisher to put out fires like the ones caused by wood and

paper. But water cannot be used to put out fires caused by petrol. Why?

15. Use of catalytic converters have proved to be reliable and effective in reducing harmful emissions from motor vehicles. What is the negative impact of its use?

16. Why is ozone widely used in the purification of drinking water?

17. In view of the polluted environment, would you like to wear mask and protective clothes everyday? Why?

18. What is a scrubber or filter? Where is it used?

19. What was the source of food before the development of agriculture?

20. Why is it necessary to level the soil after ploughing?

21. If wheat is sown in the kharif season, what would happen? Discuss.

22. Why are viruses considered to be on the borderline of living and non-living?

23. Which bird is known for its longest migration?

24. What will happen if we go on cutting trees?

25. Why should paper be saved?

26. Are the cells in an elephant larger than the cells in a rat?

27. What will happen when a cell is kept in a medium containing salt solution?

28. Why do plant cells need cell wall?

29. Why does a leaf appear green?

30. What is gestation?

31. What is brooding?

32. How Dolly was produced?

33. Can the process of a child changing into an adult be called metamorphosis?

34. Why do you think it is necessary for frogs and fishes to lay so many eggs?

35. Why is it that cats always produce several kittens, whereas human beings produce only one child at a time?

36. Why do acne and pimples appear during adolescent period?

37. What is Adam's apple?

38. What are sex hormones? Why are they named so? State their function.

Explanatory Answers

1. Force and Pressure

👉 Multiple Choice Questions

1. (A) Kicking is a pushing action while the others are pulling actions.

2. (C) Chemical energy is not a force.

3. (A) Since, the force is applied in the direction of motion of the object, the speed of the object will increase.

4. (C) In the absence of a force, a body will remain at rest (static object) or move with uniform velocity.

5. (D) We apply certain force to tear a paper. The shape of the paper changes after it is repeatedly torn into pieces.

6. (C) Frictional force between two surfaces tends to decrease the speed of a moving object.

7. (B) The electrostatic force is a non-contact force.

8. (B) Atmospheric pressure is caused by the weight of air molecules surrounding the earth.

9. (A) The pressure exerted by a liquid increases with depth.

10. (D) Thrust is the total force applied on a given area. It is given as the product of pressure and area.

11. (B) The weight of a body is balanced by the upthrust of water. Hence, the net force acting on a body is zero and so this helps the body float.

12. (B) When a ball is falling freely from a height, the net force is not equal to zero.

13. (B) When we suck air from pipe, atmospheric pressure pushes the liquid juice up to fill the vacuum and it comes up.

14. (D) A magnet attracts a magnetic material thereby making it move from rest. There may be a temporary change in the shape or size. But there is no change in the chemical composition.

15. (B) The water at a height flows down due to pressure and gravitational force.

16. (C) Water pressure increases with an increase in the depth of the sea which effects the diver's ears.

17. (C) The barometer is used to measure atmospheric pressure of a place.

18. (C) For a body to be in equilibrium or at rest, the vector sum of all forces must be zero.

19. (C) The suit (known as scuba suit) is pressurized to counter balance the heavy pressure in deep sea.

20. (D) The magnitude of non-contact force depends on the distance between two bodies, mass and chemical composition of the two bodies.

21. (D) When a rubber sucker is pressed on any surface, most of the air between its cup and the surface escapes out. The sucker sticks to the surface because of the atmospheric pressure which acts on it.

22. (A) An archer uses his strength (muscular force) to pull a bow.

23. (D) When a bowling ball is made to slide by the exertion of force, there will be a change in the position of the stationary pins.

24. (A) For throwing a stone, we need to apply a pushing force.

25. (A) $Pressure = \dfrac{Thrust}{Unit\ area}$. If the area of the cross section is high, then low pressure is exerted due to thrust. In the case of wide tyres of a heavy vehicle, the pressure exerted by the tyres is less on the road.

👉 Previous Contest Questions

1. (B) Options (A), (C) and (D) are due to application of a force. Bursting of a

balloon is due to expansion beyond the elastic limit of the balloon material.

2. (A) The weight of the man is the force applied by him on the stool.

3. (D) Statements (A), (B) and (C) are true.

    The sun lights up only half of the moon (not complete moon) at any one time. This is because moon is also a sphere like the sun.

4. (C) A book remains at rest on a table. Force exerted by the book on the table, is the same as the force exerted by the table on the book.

5. (D) Since, weight is the result of gravitational force acting on an object, there is no gravitational force acting on the astronaut and so, the weight of an astronaut in outer space will be zero.

6. (C) Our internal body pressure is equal to the atmospheric pressure. Hence, we do not feel the atmospheric pressure.

7. (D) The gravitational force for a falling body is along the direction of motion. Hence, its speed increases continuously till it touches the ground.

8. (A) The given block is a cuboid. For different orientations of faces, different areas of contact exist. Hence, pressure exerted by the block is not the same in all the cases of orientation. Pressure is thrust per unit area.

9. (A) As height increases, air pressure decreases. The figures in ascending order of heights is sea beach, high building and mountain top. Hence, ascending order of air pressure is mountain top (i), high building (ii) and sea beach (iii).

10. (B) In a spirit level, the pressure of the liquid that acts on the air bubble in all directions is balanced when the surface is horizontal. When it is inclined, the pressure is unbalanced which results in the movement of the air bubble to the right side.

2. Friction

☞ **Multiple Choice Questions**

1. (A) Frictional force is always between two surfaces in contact with each other.

2. (C) Sliding friction is less than the friction that builds up before sliding, i.e., static friction. Hence, sliding friction is less than 7 N.

3. (C) Glass has comparatively a better polished and regular surface and so, it has the least friction.

4. (C) The use of ball bearings causes rolling friction which is much less than the sliding friction.

5. (B) Friction is desirable to stop or reduce speed of a speeding vehicle. When the brakes are applied in a speeding vehicle, they rub against the wheels in motion. Due to the friction between the brakes and wheels, the speed of vehicle is reduced or it may come to stop.

6. (B) Powder is a lubricant and reduces friction. Hence, for decreasing friction, carrom board is usually powdered before playing.

7. (A) Rolling reduces friction. Rolling friction is the least amongst the three kinds of frictions, rolling, sliding and static friction.

8. (B) The frictional force exerted by fluids is called drag.

9. (C) A streamlined body reduces drag (friction) during motion.

10. (B) For the given surfaces static friction is somewhat greater than sliding friction as well as rolling friction. It is easier to roll than to slide. Hence, sliding friction is greater than rolling friction. The decreasing order of magnitude of friction is static, sliding and rolling.

11. (C) Rolling friction is much less than sliding friction. So, rolling a drum is easier.

12. (D) Due to the very high speed of meteor when it enters the earth's atmosphere, the heat produced by the friction of air is very large which causes the meteor to burn.

13. (A) Due to increased friction, greater frictional heat is produced in the match stick which thus lights up easily.

14. (B) Spikes in the shoes increase friction and prevent slipping.

15. (C) When we push the ground with our feet, the friction provides a forward reaction to our push and makes us move forward. (Walking on slippery ground is difficult because the frictional force is not enough to prevent slipping).

16. (D) Statement (A), (B) and (C) are correct.

17. (B) Friction opposes the relative motion of objects. In its absence, a moving object will not stop.

18. (D) The wearing out of the soles of shoes is a disadvantage of friction.

19. (C) Leaves falling from a tree onto the ground is due to the effect of gravitational force and not due to frictional force.

20. (B) Since, rolling friction is less than sliding friction, the tyres are made circular instead of flat.

21. (B) Sound is produced due to increased frictional force between the two surfaces. Oil is used as a lubricant to reduce frictional force in machines.

22. (D) The coin will stop because of friction exerted by the surface of the table on the coin.

23. (A) While walking on ice, one should take small steps to avoid slipping as smaller steps ensure larger friction.

24. (D) It will be difficult to sit on a chair without friction. In the other two cases too, friction is useful.

25. (A) Friction can be decreased by making the surfaces smooth.

☞ **Previous Contest Questions**

1. (B) Sliding friction is required to keep the object moving with the same speed. Once the applied force overcomes the static friction, the object starts moving.

2. (D) Holding a glass, writing on a paper and sitting on a chair are the activities which are not possible without friction.

3. (C) Ice offers the least friction as compared to water and road surfaces.

4. (C) The correct measure of air pressure in the tyres provides an air cushion to reduce rolling friction.

5. (A) Friction exerted by water is much less than that exerted by a solid. Hence, it takes more time to stop a ship in water.

6. (C) Due to larger surface area, the feather faces more air resistance (friction by air) and hence slows down, while the coin moves faster and touches the ground faster.

7. (C) When we walk on the road, the friction between the soles of our shoes and the road wears out the soles.

8. (C) In the absence of friction (no opposing motion), a moving object will keep on moving. In this case, the ball will oscillate between points 'P' and 'Q' due to the action of gravitational force.

9. (A) Friction is the relative motion between two surfaces in contact. So, a body has zero force of friction when it is at rest, i.e. when no force is applied on it.

10. (C) A person will not be able to climb a mountain if frictional force i.e., a contact force is absent.

11. (B) Frictional force is the relative force between two surfaces in contact. The motion of body X will be in the direction of pushing force. Frictional force Y acts in a direction opposite to the direction of motion.

12. (A) As both the blocks have the same mass, the friction depending on the weight of the blocks is the same and does not affect friction. Friction depends on the nature of the surfaces and sand paper is rougher than the ice block. Ice block offers the least friction than sand paper block. Hence, ice block reaches the bottom of the tray first.

13. (D) Smooth surfaces like glass offer least resistance as the friction produced is less. It is easy to move the weight on a glass surface as it is smoother than other materials.

Hence, the reading on this scale would be the smallest.

14. (D) Friction plays an important role in the striking of a match stick, playing snooker and writing on the black board.

15. (A) Friction is the relative force between two surfaces in contact, which causes the decrease in the movement of a body or sometimes may even prevent the motion.

3. Sound

☞ **Multiple Choice Questions**

1. (C) In a wave (like sound wave), the particles of the medium, the source nor the medium do not travel. It is the disturbance (energy) which travels along the path.

2. (A) The speed of sound in ascending order is minimum in gases, lesser in liquids and maximum in solids.

   Gas (air) - 330 - 340 m/s

   Liquid (water) - 1500 m/s

   Solid (steel) - 5000 m/s.

3. (C) The velocity of sound in solids (railway tracks) is faster than that in air.

4. (A) A person is identified by the sound which is characterised by its amplitude.

5. (A) Sound is produced by larynx or voice box.

6. (D) The number of oscillations per second is called the frequency of oscillation, i.e. 50 Hz.

7. (C) Sound travels the fastest in solids, less in liquids and the least in gases.

8. (C) Thunder is heard later because the speed of light (flash) is much greater (3×10^8 m s^{-1}) than the speed of sound (330 m s^{-1}).

9. (C) Two vocal cords are stretched across the larynx in such a way that it leaves a narrow slit between them for the passage of air. The length of vocal cords and the width of the slit is different in men, women, children, thus producing different sounds.

10. (B) Frequency = 1/time period.

    = 1/unit of time = second^{-1}

11. (A) The loudness or intensity of sound depends on its amplitude. The larger the amplitude, the louder is the sound produced.

12. (A) Pitch of sound depends on its frequency.

13. (D) Birds produce sounds by means of a ring of cartilage called syrinx, present at the beginning of their wind pipe.

14. (C) Musical sound is produced by regular vibrations whereas noise is produced by irregular vibrations.

15. (D) Noise pollution is hazardous to health in many ways. Insomnia (lack of sleep), hypertension (high blood pressure) and hearing impairment (temporary or permanent hearing problem) are the effects of noise pollution.

16. (D) Human beings can hear only within the range of 20 Hz to 20 kHz. So, 100 kHz (1,00, 000 Hz) cannot be heard.

17. (D) The three delicate bones in the middle ear are the hammer, the anvil and the stirrup.

18. (A) The nerve that carries the signals from the ear to the brain is called the auditory nerve.

19. (D) Vocal cords are a band of muscles within the larynx. These muscles vibrate to produce the sound.

20. (A) Frequency is the number of vibrations that pass through a point in space in one second by a body.

21. (D) A tuning fork always produces vibrations of the same frequency.

22. (D) A musical note is characterised by loudness, pitch, timbre (quality).

23. (A) In wind instruments, the frequency of the sound depends on the length of the air column.

24. (A) When we tighten the strings of a guitar, the frequency of vibration increases and high frequency sound has a high pitch.

25. (D) Pitch is the characteristic of sound that depends on the frequency of sound. Higher the pitch, greater is the frequency of the sound. Hence, higher the pitch, higher is the frequency.

☞ **Previous Contest Questions**

1. (D) The fork will vibrate with a greater amplitude when it is hit hard. Transfer of

this high energy will create higher amplitude on the surface of water.

2. (B) The vibrations produced in the air while blowing a whistle produces sound.

3. (A) The longer the vibrating material, the slower is the oscillation of scale and hence, low sound is produced. Shortening the length of the scale causes it to move up and down quickly producing a higher pitched (frequency) sound.

4. (A) Frequency α $\sqrt{tension}$. So, it increa-ses.

5. (D) As there is no atmosphere on the moon, sound does not travel through vacuum.

6. (C) A vibrating body which produces sound of a frequency higher than 2,00,000 Hz is audible to dolphins, bats, etc.

7. (A) The loudness of sound is expressed in a unit called decibel (dB). Loudness is also proportional to the square of the amplitude of vibration producing the sound. Thus, dB expresses both loudness and amplitude.

8. (C) The sensation of hearing is interpreted by brain through the pitch of the sound received.

9. (C) Sound can get reflected a number of times before reaching us. In multiple reflections of sound waves, they add up and the loudness increases. In a stethoscope, the sound of a patients's heart beat is guided along the tube to the doctor's ears by multiple reflections.

10. (B) The frequency of the sound wave in water will be more than that in air.

4. Chemical Effects of Electric Current

👉 **Multiple Choice Questions**

1. (D) Current is the flow of charge.

2. (D) In electrolytic solutions, electrolyte splits into positive and negative ions. The charge is moved through ions.

3. (B) Insulators are substances that do not conduct electricity.

4. (A) Wood is an insulator while iron, graphite and silver are good conductors of electricity.

5. (B) An LED has two leads. One lead is slightly longer than the other. The longer lead is always connected to a positive terminal of the battery while the shorter lead is always connected to a negative terminal of the battery.

In circuit (B) switch is present and is in its ON position. Only this makes the LED glow.

6. (B) In a cell, chemical energy is converted into electrical energy.

7. (D) The characteristic of an electrolyte is that it should be able to form positive and negative ions.

8. (D) Citric acid is present in the lemon juice which acts as an electrolyte.

9. (D) The electrolyte in a dry cell is ammonium chloride.

10. (D) In a dry cell, metal cap on the carbon rod acts as a positive terminal.

11. (A) The common dry cell produces a voltage of 1.5 V

12. (A) When electric current flows through a conductor, some amount of electrical energy is converted into heat energy.

13. (A) Nichrome is an alloy of nickel and chromium.

14. (A) Electrolysis is the splitting of a compound using electricity.

15. (B) Due to the heating effect of current, the filament of the bulb gets heated to a high temperature and it starts glowing.

16. (D) LED's are extensively used to replace bulbs because they consume less electricity, have longer life and have more power.

17. (C) Sea water is saline and so, it is a good conductor of electricity.

18. (B) Magnetic effect of current is responsible for the deflection of a compass needle in an electric field.

19. (D) Electroplating is the most common industrial application of chemical effects of electric current as are galvanising and anodising.

20. (D) Distilled water or pure water is a bad conductor of electricity.

Explanatory Answers

21. (C) Tin, being less reactive than iron, is used for coating cans meant for storing food items.

22. (C) To protect iron from corrosion and rust, it is coated with zinc.

23. (D) Zinc can be better than tin for protecting iron from rusting because, zinc being highly electropositive can prevent rusting even when the layer is broken.

24. (B) An LED glows even when a weak electric current flows through it.

25. (B) Vinegar is a good conductor of electricity. Hence, X is vinegar.

☞ **Previous Contest Questions**

1. (A) In a cell, by convention, charge is taken to be flowing from positive electrode to negative electrode.

2. (B) In metals, the attractive force on outermost electrons towards nucleus is feeble due to which they become free from atom when they get a little energy from outside. Such electrons are free to move anywhere inside the metal, but they are not free to move outside the metal.

3. (A) Cans used for storing soft drinks or food items are usually electroplated with tin because tin is less reactive than the base metal with which the can is made of. Tin does not contaminate the food or soft drink. It also does not get corroded.

4. (B) Anions move towards anode as they are negatively charged.

5. (B) A bulb does not glow when the probes are hanging in air, because air is a bad conductor of electricity.

6. (D) Since, tin is less reactive than iron, iron vessels are coated with tin to prevent rusting. Thus, food does not come into contact with iron and is protected from getting spoiled.

7. (B) The process of depositing a layer of any desired metal on another metal by passing electricity is called electroplating. The iron plate in the experiment is being coated with copper.

8. (B) Electroplating is the process of depositing a layer of a desired metal on another material by passing electric current.

9. (C) Acids are good conductors of electricity. Most of the liquids which conduct electricity are solutions of acids, bases and salts.

10. (A) Two like charges each of 3C experience a force of repulsion between them. A force of attraction exists between two unlike charges or between a charged and an uncharged body.

5. Some Natural Phenomena

☞ **Multiple Choice Questions**

1. (A) The force of attraction or repulsion between two charged bodies is called electrostatic force.

2. (B) During electrification by friction, one body loses electrons and gets positive charge and another gains these electrons and gets an equal amount of negative charge.

3. (A) During thunderstorm and lightning, no open place is safe. If you are travelling by car, you are safe inside with the windows and doors of the vehicle closed. The rubber tyres of the cars are non-conductors, so you will be safer inside the car.

All other options (tree, pole) have greater chances of electrocution.

(A house or a building is a safe place too.)

4. (A) Electric charge is measured in 'coulombs'.

5. (A) The charge on the ebonite rod rubbed with fur is negative (as it gains electrons). The charge on the glass rod rubbed with silk is positive (as it loses electrons). So, when these two rods are brought close to each other, they attract, since unlike charges attract each other.

6. (A) Lightning rods are made up of iron or copper (good conductors).

7. (A) Electroscope is a device used for detecting and testing charges of small magnitude in a body.

They are of two types - the pith ball electroscope and the gold leaf electroscope.

8. (D) A lightning conductor is a metallic device installed on tall buildings to protect them from lightning striking the building during a thunderstorm. The charge from the lightning gets 'attracted' to the conductor. All the charge then flows through it to the ground instead of to the building.

9. (B) When a glass rod is rubbed with silk cloth, it loses electrons and acquires positive charge.

10. (D) The process of a charge being conducted from a charged body to the earth is called earthing.

Earthing protects us from electrical shocks due to leakage of electrical current and from lightning during a thunderstorm and rain.

11. (A) The electrical charges generated by rubbing two objects are static and they do not move by themselves.

12. (D) Crust is the uppermost layer of the earth exposed to the atmosphere.

13. (C) Neutrons bear no charge upon them and they are neutral.

14. (A) The discharge of static electricity produces a spark.

15. (D) Electrical charge passes through a conductor.

16. (C) The accumulated negative and positive electric charges combine to produce streaks of bright light/ lightning.

17. (D) Squatting low on the ground will make you the smallest target to be struck. In all other cases, you are exposed to the atmosphere.

18. (D) Japan is most prone to earthquakes. People of Japan construct their buildings in such a way that these can withstand major tremors.

19. (B) Moving air is called wind. It flows from areas of higher pressure to areas of lower pressure.

20. (D) A body can be charged by conduction, induction and friction.

21. (C) An earthquake is a sudden shaking or trembling of earth. It is so sudden that it cannot be predicted in advance.

22. (A) The seismic or fault zones are most prone to earthquakes.

23. (B) The power of an earthquake is expressed in terms of its magnitude on a scale called Richter scale.

24. (A) In India, earthquakes most likely occur in Gujarat.

25. (B) The jumping of electrons between the two patches of clouds bearing different charges results in a big spark. The spark is seen as a flash of lightning.

👉 **Previous Contest Questions**

1. (C) Like charges repel and unlike charges attract each other.

2. (D) Lightning affects radio and T.V. signals resulting in the disturbance in the sound and picture clarity. It also affects the telephone wires and cause death of people when sparks of lightning fall on them.

3. (D) Statement (A), (B) and (C) list out the uses of lightning.

4. (B) The energy contained in the gaseous form (vapour) is more than the energy contained in the liquid form (water). Therefore, when vapour changes to water it loses some heat.

5. (C) A glass rod when rubbed with silk acquires positive charge.

6. (B) On the earth, the outer most layer "lithosphere" includes the crust and the mantle.

It is fragmented into tectonic plates, which move independently relative to one another. This movement of lithospheric plates is described as plate tectonics.

7. (C) Richter scale is not a linear scale. It is a logarithmic scale. A difference in magnitude of '2' implies a multiplication factor of 100.

8. (A) The outer layer of the earth, on which we live is called the crust. The thickest part of the earth's crust is the continent.

9. (D) An earthquake is usually caused by the movement of earth's plates. Apart from this, it is also caused by a meteor hitting the earth, volcanic eruption and underground nuclear explosion.

10. (D) The way a rock responds to stress depends on its temperature, the speed of stress applied and the confining pressure on the rock.

6. Light

👉 Multiple Choice Questions

1. (A) When light is incident on a rough surface, irregular reflection takes place, hence the image formed is not clear.

2. (A) Glass is coated with silver.

3. (B) An object is visible only when reflected light from the object reaches the retina of our eyes.

4. (A) The phenomenon of light in which, light is reflected or bounced back into the same medium is called reflection.

5. (C) The perpendicular drawn to the reflecting surface of a mirror at the point of incidence is called 'normal'.

    The point on the reflecting surface where the light ray is incident is called the point of incidence.

6. (C) When two mirrors are kept parallel to each other, an infinite number of images can be seen.

7. (A) The angle of incidence = the angle of reflection. So, the angle of reflection is 80°.

8. (D) A concave mirror is used by E.N.T. doctors to get a magnified image of internal organs like ear, nose and throat.

9. (A) If two plane mirrors are inclined at an angle of 60°, then

    $n = \dfrac{360}{60} - 1 = 5$ images are formed.

10. (B) In reflection of light, $\angle i = 50°$ and $\angle i = \angle r$ = the angle between incident ray and reflected ray = 50° + 50° = 100°

11. (D) We use plane mirrors to see ourselves, because the image formed by a plane mirror is virtual, erect and of the same size.

12. (B) When a light ray is reflected from the reflecting surface, the incident ray, the reflected ray and the normal lie in the same plane.

    The angle of incidence = The angle of reflection .

13. (D) The image formed by the plane mirror is laterally inverted i.e., the right side of the object appears on the left side of the image and left side of the object appears on the right side of the image.

14. (B) The two reflecting, plane mirrors arranged in a periscope are parallel to each other. The light ray from the object is incident on the first plane mirror at an angle of 45° and the reflected ray is incident on the second mirror at 45° and is then reflected at 45°, which finally reaches the retina of the eye.

15. (D) The human eye serves as a convex lens. It forms real, inverted and diminished image of an object.

16. (C) Persistance of vision is a phenomenon where the brain continues to sense the image even after the object has been removed. This lasts for 1/16th of a second.

17. (D) Cataract occurs in old age due to the given characteristics and can be cured by introducing a new artificial lens.

18. (D) The nocturnal animals need more light to see at night. The large cornea and pupil allow more light to enter into their eyes. They also have retina with large number of rods.

19. (C) $\angle i = 40°$ (given)

    $\angle i = \angle r = 40°$

    The angle between the incident ray and the reflected ray

    $= \angle i + \angle r$

    $= 40° + 40° = 80°$

20. (B) We know that for a reflected ray, the angle that the incident ray makes with the line perpendicular to the surface is equal to the angle made by the reflected ray with

this perpendicular line. N is the correct reflected ray of X.

21. (A)   In the case of a periscope, the given fact is used and is illustrated below.

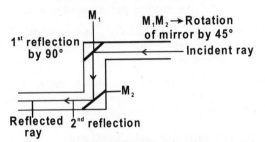

22. (C)   Object distance after shifting the object = 4 m + 0.5 m = 4.5 m

For a plane mirror;

Object distance = Image distance = 4.5 m

Distance between the object and its image = 4.5 + 4.5 = 9 m

23. (C)   The letters that are not changed when the word is seen by reflection are : X, A, M, I, A, T, I, O i.e. 8 letters.

24. (C)   The angle between the incident ray and reflected ray = $\lfloor i + \lfloor r$

From the given figure, $\lfloor i = 90 - 25$

$\lfloor i = 65^0 = \lfloor r$ and (laws of reflection)

$\lfloor i + \lfloor r = 65° + 65° = 130°$

25. (C)   The dispersion of sunlight is the splitting of white light into rays of seven different colours. Just after the rain, there are a large number of water drops in the air which act like small prisms. As the white sunlight enters these water drops, the constituents of white light of different colours are refracted by different amounts, and a band of seven colours called rainbow is formed.

Previous Contest Questions

1. (B)   T is a laterally symmetrical object and hence its image in a plane mirror would be the same as itself.

2. (C)   An ideal mirror reflects all the light.

3. (B)   Three plane mirrors are arranged at an angle to get a number of coloured images in a kaleidoscope.

4. (C)   A series of fast moving still pictures can create an illusion of movement as the eye can separate two images only when the interval of separation between them is one-sixteenth of a second. This happens due to a phenomenon called persistence of vision.

5. (C)   The inner layer of the eye called the choroid is black. This prevents internal reflections of light inside the human eye.

6. (C)   The point nearest to the eye at which an object is distinctly visible is called the near point of the eye. The distance of the near point of the eye is called the least distance of distinct vision. It varies with age. For an infant, it is 5 to 8 cm, for an adult, it is 20 to 25 cm.

7. (D)   Images are formed on the retina.

8. (C)   The image formed on the retina is real, inverted and diminished. The optic nerve transmits the inverted image to the brain which reads it as an erect image.

9. (C)   A person suffering from myopia has elongation of the eye ball. As such he cannot see distant objects clearly. A suitable concave lens can rectify the above defect, so that the image falls on the retina.

10. (C)   According to the laws of reflection, the angle of incidence is always equal to the angle of reflection.

7. Stars and the Solar System

Multiple Choice Questions

1. (D)   One light year is the distance travelled by light in one year, i.e. 9.46×10^{12} km.

2. (A)   The sun is a part of the solar system. Proxima Centauri is about 4.3 light years from the earth and nearest to the solar system.

3. (D)   Constellation is a group of stars that appear to form some kind of pattern.

4. (D)   36,000 km is the approximate height of a geostationary satellite from the earth.

5. (B)   India joined the space club on April 19, 1975 by putting into orbit Aryabhatta, a 350 kg satellite. This was done with the help of Russian rockets and from Russian soil.

On June 7, 1979, Bhaskara 1, India's second satellite was put into orbit successfully.

6. (B) Jupiter is the largest planet and it is made up of gas.

7. (A) Stars appear to move from east to west. This is because the earth rotates on its axis from west to east.

8. (D) Orion is the name of a constellation which means the hunter.

9. (C) The great red spot on Jupiter's surface is actually a huge storm .

10. (A) A spy-satellite is an earth observation satellite (or) communication satellite deployed in a low-earth orbit, for military (or) intelligence applications.

11. (C) Ceres is an asteroid that was first discovered and it is also the largest.

12. (A) The moon is not a star. It is the only natural satellite visible to us on the earth.

13. (B) The only moon in the solar system with active volcanoes is Io.

14. (D) Ganymede, one of the many moons of Jupiter, is the largest satellite in our solar system.

15. (D) Mercury, Mars, Venus and Jupiter can be seen with the naked eye.

16. (C) Natural satellites e.g., moon revolve around the earth in an elliptical orbit.

Geostationary satellites revolve around the earth in circular orbits.

17. (B) The largest of the 88 recognized constellations is Hydra. It is best seen from the southern hemisphere. The smallest constellation is Crux.

18. (A) Ozone is made up of oxygen.

19. (C) Johannes Kepler proved that the planets revolve around the sun in elliptical orbits. He also formulated the laws of planetary motion, which have been named after him.

20. (D) The time taken by our galaxy, the milky way to revolve around itself once is called a Cosmic Year (225×10^6 years).

21. (B) Between 1979 and 1999, the farthest planet from the sun was Neptune.

22. (A) The nearest galaxy to ours is Andromeda which is 2 million light years away from us.

23. (C) Venus takes maximum time of 243 days for one rotation around its own axis .

24. (A) Halley is the name of a comet which was first observed by Halley in 1986. It appears once in every 76 years.

25. (B) The sun was formed from the gravitational collapse of a giant molecular cloud 4.5 billion years ago.

☞ Previous Contest Questions

1. (C) Stars are mainly made up of hydrogen and helium.

2. (B) Edwin Hubble, an astronomer observed that the galaxies are not stationary but are moving away from each other. The larger the distance between the two galaxies, the faster they move away from each other. This led him to propose and conclude that the universe is expanding.

3. (C) The pole star is situated in the north along the axis of rotation of the earth and so its position relating to the earth always remains the same.

4. (A) The live telecast of a cricket match is possible due to geostationary satellite.

5. (A) The "sea of tranquility" is found on the moon.

6. (D) A cosmic year is the time taken by the sun to revolve around the Milky Way galaxy.

7. (A) Though mercury is closer to the sun than Venus, Venus is hotter than Mercury. The reason is that Mercury has no atmosphere and Venus has a thick atmosphere which can retain the heat.

8. (B) The closely packed part of the comet which contains solid particles, stones and frozen water is called the nucleus.

9. (A) Mercury has the shortest period of revolution. Hence, it is the fastest planet of the solar system.

10. (A) The constellation is Orion.

1. Synthetic Fibres and Plastics

☞ **Multiple Choice Questions**

1. (C) Wool is made from fleece(hair) of sheep or yak.

2. (D) Reeling is the extracting of silk threads from cocoons.

3. (C) The caterpillar secretes a protein called fibroin which hardens on exposure to air and become silk fibres.

4. (D) Nylon is the first, fully, synthetic fibre obtained from coal, air and water.

5. (C) Nylon fibre is strong, elastic and light. It is lustrous and easy to wash. So, it became very popular for making clothes.

6. (B) Jute is made from the inner fibre of the stem. Coconut fibre is the outer covering of the coconut.

7. (D) Esters are responsible for the characteristic smell of fruits.

8. (B) Spectacles are made up of glass and plastic, which are man-made.

9. (C) Mattresses are made from coconut fibres.

10. (D) The nylon thread is stronger than the cotton thread.

11. (B) Thermoplastic is a type of plastic that can be softened or bent easily by heating and hardened by cooling.

    e.g., PVC, Polythene etc.

12. (D) Plastic is non-reactive, light, strong and durable. It is easily remouldable. All these properties make plastic most convenient for its use.

13. (C) Most of the synthetic fibres are prepared from petrochemicals.

14. (D) The correct combination is :

    a - 4, b - 1, c - 2, d - 3

    (i)   Silk - Saree

    (ii) Nylon - Rope

    (iii) Acrylic - Sweater

    (iv) Plastic - Bottle

15. (A) Plastic, metal cans, etc.. are the materials which cannot be decomposed by natural processes. Hence, they are non - biodegradable.

16. (B) Polythene is formed by the polymerisation of ethylene.
    Polymerisation is a process in which molecules of the same or different compounds are joined together to form a long chain of molecules called polymers.

17. (C) The plastics which can be remoulded are called thermoplastics.

    e.g., Polythene, PVC etc.

18. (D) All synthetic products/chemicals are non-biodegradable and cannot be decomposed easily.

19. (C) Plastic when coated with melamine becomes fire proof. These materials are used for preparing fabrics for fire-men, and making kitchen ware etc.

20. (B) Terylene fibres are made up of chemical substances called esters.

21. (D) The 4R principle i.e., reduce, reuse, recycle and recover applies for plastic.

22. (B) Thermoplastics are bad conductors of heat and electricity.

23. (D) Plastic as such is not flame resistant but thermosetting plastics resist fire, non-corrosive and mouldable. They can be used for making kitchen ware.

24. (B) Natural polymers are polymers produced by living organisms. They include natural rubber and natural food stuffs. Polyester is a synthetic fibre (not a natural polymer).

25. (B) Polywool is a mixture of polyester and wool.

☞ **Previous Contest Questions**

1. (B) Nylon is made up of petrochemicals and is purely a synthetic fibre. Rayon is made of wood pulp. Cotton and flax are natural fibres.

2. (C) Differences (i) and (iii) are true of thermoplastics and thermosetts.

3. (B) Nylon is strong, elastic and light.

4. (A) Melamine is an example of thermoset plastics. Thermoset plastics are heavily cross-linked polymers and hence, they are rigid.

5. (A) The burning of synthetic polymers release smoke and toxic gases which pollute the environment.

6. (C) Thermoplastics are resistant to most of the chemicals. They are easy to burn, bend and do not conduct electricity and they consist of linear polymer chains which are linked by weak attractive forces.

7. (C) Synthetic fibres like polyesters absorb less water and dry up quickly.

8. (B) Synthetic fibres catch fire easily and melt on heating. Therefore, it is not safe to wear clothes made of synthetic fibres. So, cotton clothes are best and safe.

9. (B) Acrylic is an artificial wool.

10. (B) The use of biodegradable bags is the best method to avoid pollution.

2. Metals and Non-metals

☞ **Multiple Choice Questions**

1. (A) Metals generally have 1,2 or 3 electrons in their outermost orbit or valence shell.

    e.g., (i)   Sodium - (Na) - 2, 8, 1

    (ii) Magnesium (Mg) - 2, 8, 2

    (iii) Aluminium - (Al) - 2, 8, 3.

    The number of valence electrons in sodium, magnesium and aluminium metals are 1, 2 and 3 respectively.

2. (D) Non-metals generally contain 4,5,6,7 or 8 electrons in their outermost orbit or shell.

    (i)   Carbon – 2, 4

    (ii) Nitrogen - 2.5

    (iii) Oxygen - 2, 6

    (iv) Fluorine - 2, 7

The number of valence electrons in carbon, nitrogen, oxygen and fluorine are 4, 5, 6, 7 respectively.

3. (B) Elements which show the properties of both the metals and non-metals are called metalloids.

    e.g., antimony and arsenic

4. (A) Calcium is more reactive than magnesium. Hence, Mg can be replaced from its salt by calcium.

5. (B) Aluminium foil is prepared by beating it into sheets. i.e., property of malleability. Hence, aluminium foil is used for the given application.

6. (C) Sulphur is yellow in colour.

7. (D) Non-metals have low densities, low melting points and are poor conductors of electricity.

8. (C) Bromine is the only non-metal which exists in liquid state at room temperature.

9. (A) Copper, Mercury, Silver and Gold are less reactive than hydrogen. Hence, they cannot displace hydrogen from the compounds like dilute acids, water, etc.

10. (A) Among the given metals, sodium is a highly reactive metal, so it reacts vigorously to form salt and hydrogen.

    $$2Na + 2HCl \rightarrow 2NaCl + H_2 \uparrow$$

11. (A) Non-metals form two types of oxides, they can be acidic or neutral oxides.

12. (D) Some oxides of non-metals are neutral. e.g., CO.

13. (B) Phosphorus combines with oxygen and forms two oxides phosphorus trioxide and phosphorus pentoxide.

14. (C) Acidic oxides dissolve in water and form acids.

    Sulphur trioxide (SO_3) reacts with water and produces sulphuric acid (H_2SO_4)

    $$SO_3 + H_2O \rightarrow H_2SO_4$$

15. (B) Silver bromide, a compound of silver is used to make photographic films. When

light falls on the film, it sets up a reaction which changes silver bromide to silver.

16. (C) Crucibles are used in the laboratory to perform high temperature reactions. They should resist high heating (they should not break). For this purpose, a mixture of graphite (an allotrope of carbon) and clay is used to make crucibles.

17. (A) Sulphur is used in the process of vulcanisation. Rubber when treated with sulphur becomes harder than ordinary rubber, so it is used to make tyres.

18. (B) Gold, silver and platinum do not combine readily with other elements to form compounds, so they are called noble metals.

19. (A) Sodium has less density, hence it is soft and can be cut even with a knife.

20. (C) Metal tungsten is used as a filament in electric bulbs because it has a high melting point.

21. (D) 'K' is not a heavy metal. It is a light metal.

22. (A) The supply of nitrogen to a corrosive metal will prevent its corrosion.

23. (A) When an iron article is dipped in molten zinc, it is galvanised.

24. (B) The descending order of reactivity of metals is as follows:

$Na > Ca > Mg > Al > Zn > Fe > Sn > Pb$ [H] $Cu > Hg > Ag > Au > Pt$

By using this, we can say that in the given options, only $Na > Fe > Cu$ is the correct order.

25. (D) In the reaction of aluminium powder with dil. H_2SO_4, the products formed are aluminium sulphate and hydrogen gas.

$2Al + (dil.)\ 3H_2SO_4 \rightarrow Al_2(SO_4)_3 + 3H_2$

☞ **Previous Contest Questions**

1. (C) Metal oxides are reduced to metals.

2. (B) Gold is mixed with copper to make it hard.

3. (C) Generally, metals are ductile.

4. (B) $Zn + CuSO_4 \rightarrow Cu + ZnSO_4$.

Hence, X is zinc and Y is copper.

5. (C) All metals are good conductors of electricity, whereas insulators are bad conductors of electricity.

6. (A) When aluminium powder is heated with iron oxide, an exothermic reaction takes place with the formation of aluminium oxide and iron metal.

7. (B) Sodium and potassium are metals. They are soft and can be cut with a knife.

8. (C) The hardest substance known is diamond. Diamond is an allotrope of carbon i.e., a non-metal.

9. (B) Gold being less reactive than hydrogen is placed below hydrogen in reactivity series. It cannot produce hydrogen gas on reaction with acids.

10. (A) The reactivity of the metals given in the options is as follows:

$K > Mg > Cu > Ag$. Magnesium reacts vigorously with steam but slowly with water. Hence, X is magnesium.

3. Coal and Petroleum

☞ **Multiple Choice Questions**

1. (A) Petroleum is a fossil fuel as it is obtained by the decomposition of the remains of plants and animals under the sea over millions of years.

2. (A) Usually petroleum and natural gas occur at the same place. Petroleum occurs as liquid, whereas natural gas is in the gaseous state above petroleum.

3. (A) Petroleum is a thick, black coloured, viscous liquid which is a rich source of different, useful and expensive products like kerosene, petrol, diesel etc., as gold, hence it is called as black gold.

4. (B) The most common sources of energy used in automobiles are petroleum and diesel.

5. (C) In the oil wells along with petroleum, natural gas also exists. It comes out first when an oil well is drilled through rocks.

6. (A) Petroleum is refined by the process of fractional distillation as the constituents of petroleum products are in the liquid state and differ in their boiling points.

7. (B) During fractional distillation, crude petroleum that is obtained from the earth's crust is heated to a temperature of about 400-500 °C. The different constituents present start separating out at different heights of the fractionating column depending upon their boiling points.

8. (A) Solid fuels leave more smoke and ash on burning because they contain a large number of impurities.

9. (C) Fractional distillation is a method of separation of liquid substances based on their different boiling points.

10. (A) Gasoline is one of the products obtained during the fractional distillation of petroleum. Gasoline works as petrol. Hence, it is used as fuel in vehicles.

11. (A) When dead plants and animals get buried deep under the earth, they get decomposed by the action of anaerobic bacteria.

    Hydrogen and oxygen escape as gases leaving behind carbon. As years pass, layers of carbon atoms are added one above the other forming a stony substance called coal, this process is called carbonisation.

12. (D) Coal is of four different varieties: peat, lignite, bituminous and anthracite. Among these, peat is the low grade quality coal. It is formed during the starting stage of coal formation. It has the lowest percentage of carbon around 10%-20%.

13. (A) Anthracite is a fine quality coal. It contains the highest percentage of carbon. It contains 94-98% carbon.

14. (D) As oxygen is a supporter of combustion, fuels burn in oxygen to produce heat and light.

15. (B) Natural gas is a mixture of methane, ethane, propane, butane, carbon dioxide, nitrogen and oxygen. But methane CH_4 constitutes a major percentage of about 85.

16. (B) Gobar gas (produced by the decomposition of animal dung, domestic and agricultural waste in the presence of anaerobic bacteria) contains methane in bulk (50-68%) and other gases in relatively low proportions, i.e. CO_2 (25-35%), H_2 (1-5%), N_2 (2-7%) etc.

17. (B) Generally, gases are liquified by applying high pressure (or) low temperature. In LPG cylinders especially, the gas is liquified by applying high pressure and it is stored in cylinders.

18. (B) In fractional distillation of petroleum, the vapours with the highest boiling point cannot move up in the fractionating column, (as they have low vapour pressure). So, the liquids with high boiling points condense in the lowest (tray) portion of the fractionating tower.

19. (C) Kerosene oil is more suitable than petrol in oil lamps because kerosene oil is less volatile than petrol. It costs less and is easy to handle.

20. (B) Kerosene is mainly used as a fuel in jet engines.

21. (B) The correct combination is:

    a – 2, b – 1, c – 4, d – 3.

    Carbonisation – coal

    Destructive distillation – coke

    Cracking – hydrocarbons

    Refining – petroleum

22. (A) Petroleum gas is a mixture of ethane, propane and butane. Butane, being a major part of the composition is about 95%.

23. (C) Fly ash is a fine powder formed when large amount of coal is burnt in sufficient quantity of air in places like thermal power stations etc. The ash is carried by atmospheric air due to strong current of air in the furnace, Hence, this ash is called fly ash. It causes respiratory problems when inhaled by man.

24. (B) Biogas is formed by anaerobic degradation (fermentation) of plants and animal wastes. Hence, it is not a fossil fuel.

25. (C) Coke is a tough, porous, black substance. It is almost a pure form of carbon and used in the manufacture of steel.

👉 **Previous Contest Questions**

1. (C) Petroleum has less density than water so it floats on water. It is insoluble in water because petroleum is non-polar while water is polar.

2. (A) Fuel is said to be good if it has the following characteristics:

    (i)   Low ignition temperature.

    (ii) Low cost.

    (iii) Causing minimum pollution on burning.

    (iv) Readily available.

3. (D) Producer gas is not a good fuel because it contains nitrogen which does not burn.

4. (A) Carbon monoxide is the most harmful substance for the human body.

5. (D) A fuel should have the following characteristics to act as a rocket fuel:

    (i)   It should be light and compact.

    (ii) It should produce high energy on burning.

    (iii) It should burn rapidly.

6. (A) Biogas is produced by the decomposition of animal dung, domestic and agricultural waste in the presence of anaerobic bacteria. It contains methane in bulk (50 - 68 %) and other gases in relatively low proportions i.e. CO_2 (25 - 35 %), H_2 (1- 5 %), N_2 (2-7 %) etc.

7. (D) Water has the highest boiling point.

8. (D) Coke is almost a pure form of carbon, it is a good fuel and burns without smoke. While coal is an impure form of carbon and burns releasing smoke.

9. (C) Anthracite is by and far, the most superior quality of coal which contains 94-98% carbon. It is lustrous. It burns without smoke and gives more heat and little ash. Hence, the grading of coal from superior to inferior is Anthracite, bituminous, lignite, peat.

10. (D) Fuels can be classified on the basis of their physical state like solid, liquid and gas.

    Alcohol is an example of liquid fuel.

4. Combustion and Flame

👉 **Multiple Choice Questions**

1. (A) L.P.G. is a mixture of hydrocarbons. It consists of butane, propane and ethane but butane and propane are the two major constituents of L.P.G.

2. (B) Calorific value of a substance is the amount of heat released during the combustion of a specified amount of fuel or food.

    The calorific value is the charac-teristic of a substance.

3. (C) Natural gas has the highest calorific value of 50000 kJ/kg

    Petrol has 45000 kJ/kg

    Kerosene has 45000 kJ/kg and

    Coke has 28000 kJ/kg

4. (B) All the given substances can act as fuels but butane is considered as a good fuel because of the following characteristics:

    (i)   Exists in gaseous state

    (ii) Has high calorific value

    (iii) Does not form poisonous products during combustion

5. (C) The process of a substance burning in the presence of air with evolution of heat is called combustion.

6. (A) Fuels and hydrocarbons burn in oxygen and form CO_2 , H_2O and give out heat.

    $$CH_4 + 2O_2 \rightarrow CO_2 + 2H_2O + heat$$

7. (D) Combustion is an oxidation reaction accompanied by heat and light.

8. (B) Diamond is a non-combustible substance.

9. (D) The temperature at which a substance starts burning on heating is called ignition temperature. Highly inflammable substances have a low ignition temperature. Hence, they catch fire easily.

10. (A) A burning substance will be extinguished if the temperature falls below its ignition temperature.

11. (A) Rapid combustion is a form of combustion in which large amounts of heat and light energy are released. Candle shows rapid combustion, whereas cracker and white phosphorous come under explosion and spontaneous combustion respectively.

12. (B) The combustion in which heat, light and sound are produced is known as explosive combustion.

13. (C) The correct combination is

a – 3, b – 4, c – 2, d – 1

(i) Dark inner zone – Unburnt vapours of wax

(ii) Blue zone – Complete combustion

(iii) Luminous zone – Partial combustion

(iv) Non-luminous zone – Hottest part (no carbon)

14. (D) The blue zone in L.P.G. flame indicates the hottest zone where complete combustion takes place.

15. (A) Natural gas consists of methane, ethane, propane etc., of which methane forms major composition of about 95% .

16. (C) The Bergius Process is a very simple process for converting brown coal completely into crude oil. It was invented by Dr. Friedrich Bergius.

In this process, brown coal, also known as lignite is powdered and mixed with heavy oil and heated with hydrogen under high pressure of about 200-250 atm. and a temperature of about 748 K in the presence of iron oxide as catalyst.

The vapours on condensation give a liquid resembling crude oil. This is called synthetic petrol, which on fractional distillation gives petrol (gasoline).

17. (D) (i) Wood — 17000 to 22000 kJ/kg

(ii) Coal — 25000 to 33000 kJ/kg

(iii) Petrol — 45000 kJ/kg

(iv) Natural gas — 50000 kJ/kg

The correct order of the increasing order of calorific values is : (ii),(iii),(i),(iv).

18. (A) When a fuel (carbon) undergoes incomplete combustion, carbon monoxide is formed. It is a poisonous gas and fatal, if inhaled.

19. (D) 1 kg of fuel when burnt gives 20,000 joules of heat energy.

50,000 joules of heat energy will be produced by 2.5 kg of fuel as given below.

1 kg fuel produces 20 kJ kg^{-1} heat

? fuel produces 50 kJ kg^{-1} heat

$$= \frac{50000}{20000} = 2.5 \text{ kg}$$

20. (A) Combustion is burning of a substance in the presence of oxygen.During this process heat energy is released, it is therefore an oxidation and exothermic reaction.

21. (D) Though hydrogen is a highly combustible gas, because of its high calorific value, it is used as rocket fuel, for cutting and welding metals in the form of oxyhydrogen flame and as a car fuel under stringent safety conditions.

22. (C) Energy released by 12 kg of L.P.G. in 30 days

= No. of kg of gas utilised by a family in 30 days $\times$ calorific value of gas.

$$= \frac{12}{30} \times 50 = 20 \text{ kJ / day.}$$

Therefore, energy consumed per day:

= 20,000 joules/day.

23. (B) Inflammable substances have very low ignition temperatures, so they catch fire easily .

   e.g., alcohol, ether, carbon disulphide, benzene, synthetic fibres etc.

24. (D) Incomplete combustion of a fuel results in the formation of unburnt carbon and some poisonous gases like 'CO' and oxides of nitrogen which cause air pollution leading to many respiratory problems.

25. (C) Carbon dioxide is the best extinguisher for inflammable materials like petrol, because it is heavier than oxygen, it covers fire like a blanket. Since, the contact between the fuel and oxygen is cut off, the fire is controlled. Secondly, it does not harm the electrical equipment.

   It can also be used to put out fires involving electrical equipment.

👉 **Previous Contest Questions**

1. (C) The type of fuel involved in the combustion determines the type of flame (colour and temperature of a flame varies with the chemical composition of the fuel).

2. (B) Global warming may cause glaciers to melt, which may lead to a rise in the sea level and thus submerge low lying areas.

3. (C) Butane is an odourless gas, so it is mixed with mercaptan such that if the gas leaks in air, it can be easily detected due to its peculiar choking smell and prevents it from explosion.

4. (D) The availability of hydrogen is less and also forms an explosive mixture with air or oxygen and causes explosion if it leaks out. Its storage and transport are difficult.

5. (A) Gaps are left in between logs of wood placed in chullahs to allow free movement of air, which helps in combustion.

6. (B) For spontaneous combustion to take place, a substance should have low ignition temperature:

   e.g., The ignition temperature of phosphorus is 35° C.

7. (D) A tank filled with petrol implies there is no air/oxygen inside the tank. As there is no supporter of combustion, burning of petrol does not takes place though spark is brought nearer to it .

8. (C) Diesel will give out maximum amount of heat by complete combustion when compared with wood, coal and biogas.

9. (D) A fire needs fuel, air (oxygen which supports combustion), and heat to raise the temperature of the fuel beyond ignition temperature.

10. (B) It is not the luminous zone but the non-luminous zone of the flame that has a very high temperature.

5. Pollution of Air and Water

👉 **Multiple Choice Questions**

1. (C) In air, the composition of nitrogen is about 78%, while 21% by composition is oxygen, 0.9% constitutes rare gases and 0.03% is CO_2.

2. (C) Chlorofluorocarbons lead to the depletion of ozone layer.

3. (A) Air pollution is not caused by increasing forest reserves.

4. (D) NO_2 is not a general pollutant of air.

5. (A) Carbon dioxide causes global warming, which is the same as greenhouse effect. Hence, the gas is called greenhouse gas.

6. (B) The release of carbon particles and smoke from factories decreases the rate of photosynthesis in plants.

7. (C) Oxides of sulphur i.e., sulphur dioxide and sulphur trioxide gases present in air combine with moisture and form acids, which come down along with rain water. This is called acid rain.

8. (C) Heat reflected from the earth's surface is trapped in the atmosphere. This is referred to as the greenhouse effect.

9. (C) Sewage comes from the houses not from factories. Poisonous chemicals come from factories.

10. (C) SO_2 is regarded as an air pollutant.

Explanatory Answers

11. (A) Sulphur dioxide in air affects the skin and the lungs of human beings.

12. (B) Burning of leaded petrol in automobiles releases lead particles into the air and causes pollution.

13. (C) Ozone layer present in the atmosphere protects us from UV rays by preventing them from reaching the earth.

14. (A) Monuments of marble can be destroyed by acid rain because acid corrodes calcium carbonate (marble). The pollutants in air that cause acid rain are oxides of sulphur and nitrogen.

15. (B) Aerosols are the sources of major pollutants like CFC's.

16. (C) A major air pollutant in cities like Delhi and Kolkata is suspended particulate matter.

17. (A) Automobiles use catalytic converters like platinum. These acts as catalysts to convert CO to CO_2.

18. (B) A combination of smoke and fog is smog.

19. (A) CO_2 traps heat and does not allow it to escape into space. Hence, if there is no CO_2 in the atmosphere, the earth's temperature would be less than the present.

20. (C) Potable water should be free from sodium, calcium and magnesium. Potable water should be clean, colourless and odourless, free from bacteria and must contain dissolved oxygen and carbon dioxide.

21. (B) Ammonia is not present in vehicular exhaust emissions.

22. (D) The main cause of water pollution in India is the discharge of untreated sewage and industrial waste.

23. (A) Ozone layer is present in the stratosphere.

24. (C) The main cause of sulphur dioxide emissions is the combustion of fuels like coal in power plants.

25. (D) Reducing the amount of waste formed, reusing the waste and recycling the waste contribute towards better waste management.

☞ **Previous Contest Questions**

1. (D) Smoking in public places affects the health of an individual and not the environment. Air pollution can be reduced by

    (i) burning household rubbish in incinerators,

    (ii) using catalytic converters in motor vehicles and

    (iii) fixing electric precipitators to factory chimneys.

2. (D) Due to global warming, there is

    (i) an increase in the water level in the sea,

    (ii) glaciers on mountain peaks melt due to increase of earth's temperature by 0.5° C and

    (iii) there is a decrease in food production by plants.

3. (D) The bio-indicator of air pollution is lichens. Lichens are a good indicator of the level of pollution as some lichens are very sensitive and cannot grow where air pollution is above a certain level.

4. (B) By the term 'conserving the environment' we mean that the quality of the environment should not be lowered.

5. (D) Pollution from the burning of fossil fuels can be reduced by all the three given methods.

6. (C) Global warming is caused when carbon dioxide is released into the air.

7. (D) Sewage water is purified for recycling by the action of non-biodegradable chemicals.

8. (C) Trapping of heat radiations by earth's atmosphere is known as green house effect.

9. (A) Electrical power stations use water to make steam to run the turbines and generate electricity. The used steam or superheated water which is of no use is released directly into water bodies. As aquatic animals are cold blooded, they cannot withstand excess heat and die. Aquatic plants carry out photosynthesis and release oxygen into the water. They too die and cause a decrease of oxygen in water. Points (iii) and (iv) are caused due to eutropication.

10. (A) N_2 is not an air pollutant.

1. Food Production and Management

☞ **Multiple Choice Questions**

1. (C) Agriculture is the science of growing crops.It covers all the activities connected with cultivation and farm animals.

2. (C) In the given sequence X represents the process of manuring.

3. (D) The use of machinery in agriculture increases the quantity of crop and gets the job done faster.

4. (C) Genetic engineering involves combining desirable characteristic features and transferring them into plants and multiply them.

5. (A) The correct sequence of steps to develop a new variety of plant are as follows. T - Development of the gene variation, R - selection, P - evaluation, Q - multiplication of improved seeds and S - Distribution of improved seeds.

6. (D) The optimum use of land for agriculture will improve the quantity of food production. Crop rotation and mixed cropping methods will improve the quality. Education and guidance by experts will be a great help too.

7. (C) Rhizobium bacteria are present in root nodules.

8. (D) Breeding livestock on oil palm plantations and planting many types of crops on a small area are examples of an integrated cultivation system.

9. (D) By practising efficient land management and continous researches in the field of agriculture, increase in food production and helps to meet the demands of an increasing population.

10. (D) Genetic engineering produce high quality traits in livestock and poultry, application of synthetic chemicals imrpove soil fertility and the using of agromachineryfor planting, harvesting and collecting agriculture produce are the modern technology in agriculture.

11. (D) Shifting cultivation and excessive use of chemical fertilizers will result in the loss of soil fertility.

12. (A) Rice is a kharif crop.

13. (C) Excessive irrigation causes salinisation of soil.

14. (D) Bacteria and algae play an important role in the nitrogen cycle.

15. (C) The nitrogen cycle maintains the concentration of nitrogen in air. It ensures a continous source of protein.

16. (C) Grain stocked for emergencies is called buffer stock.

17. (B) The sprinkler system of irrigation controls water supply, and water is distributed uniformly all over the field.Prevents wastage of water and loss of soil minerals.

18. (B) Rice requires more irrigation.

19. (D) The order of agricultural practices that are followed while doing cultivation is: ploughing, levelling, manuring, sowing, irrigation, harvesting.

20. (D) Ploughing loosens the soil and allows the roots to penetrate easily.It promotes the growth of useful soil bacteria that need air for respiration. When the soil is hard, plant growth is not as good.

21. (C) Monocropping does not improve soil fertility because the soil loses certain nutrients. Farmer should practise crop rotation to increase soil fertility. leguminous plants enrich the soil.

22. (D) Field fallow practices keep the fields free for a season to replenish the lost nutrients.

23. (D) Winnowing is the separation of chaff from grain. In most villages in India, winnowing is done by hand, with the help of winds. The wind blows away the chaff. The grain is then collected. Modern farmers use machines to separat chaff from grain.

24. (A) The practice of growing crops like legumes in one season and cereals the next season, on the same land, is

Explanatory Answers

called crop rotation.It helps to enrich the soil.Farmers get good crops for harvesting.

25. (B) Bacteria present in the root nodules of the leguminous crop plants have the ability to fix atmospheric nitrogen to form nitrogen compounds. Some of these are used by leguminous plants and the rest are left in the soil to enrich it.

26. (C) The rotation of crops replinshes the lost fertility of the soil. Weeds and pests are controlled by weedicides and pesticides.

27. (A) Transplantation enables us to select better and healthy seedlings for cultivation of rice.

28. (C) Chemical fertilizers are made of chemicals.

29. (A) Eutrophication means toxication of water by fertilizers.

30. (C) Paddy crops get attacked by gundhi bug.

31. (D) The farming of high yielding varieties of crops give less fodder, requires frequent weeding and higher inputs.

32. (C) Green revolution depends on fertilizers, weedicides and pesticides.

33. (D) Increase in milk production, proper utilisation of animal wastes, protection of animals against diseases are advantages of animal husbandry.

34. (B) White revolution is also called operation flood.

35. (D) Artificial insemination by a pedigree bull only, super ovulation of a high production cow only, embryo transplantation only are the process involved in production of super milk cows.

36. (A) Napier grass is used us roughage.

37. (B) The correct combination is : Kharif crops - paddy, rabi crops - wheat, tilling - ploughing and combine - harvesting.

38. (B) A leveller is used for levelling the field.

39. (A) A harrow is used to remove weeds in a field and also to level the wet field before transplantation.

40. (A) Ploughing helps in the loosening of soil. It is first and foremost agricultural operation carried by the farmer. After ploughing, soil becomes porous and soft.

☞ **Previous Contest Questions**

1. (B) Amaranthus is a weed plant that grows along with every crop.

2. (B) Seed drill is used to sow seeds.

3. (D) Fungicide solution is used to treat seeds to prevent seed - borne diseases.

4. (B) Nitrogen is an essential element required to synthesise proteins.

5. (B) In the given nitrogen cycle X represents nitrates.

6. (D) Field fallow keep the fields free for a season to replenish the lost nutrients.

7. (C) Blue green algae when added to a barren field can support crop growth.

8. (D) The correct sequence in farming is tillling - manuring - sowing - irrigation.

9. (D) Leaving the land or field uncultivated is called field fallow.

10. (C) Wheat is a rabi crop.

2. Cell

☞ **Multiple Choice Questions**

1. (A) A nerve cell is the longest cell in the human body.

2. (C) Connective tissue includes blood.

3. (D) A cell wall and vacuole are absent in animal cells.

4. (D) The iris of the eye, uterus and bronchi contain smooth muscles.

5. (D) Nervous system consists of brain, spinal cord and nerves.

6. (B) Connective tissue give support to the body, and defends with pathogens and stores food in the body.

7. (C) Epithelial tissue forms the outer protective covering all over the body and also lines body cavities.

8. (B) The nervous tissue is present in the brain, the spinal cord and nerves.

9. (B) Golgi bodies are usually called dictyosomes in plants. The main function of golgi body is to secrete digestive enzymes through membrane-bound vesicles.

10. (D) Vacuoles are called the store houses of the cell and store water, food and the excreted substances of the cell.

11. (D) The carbohydrate present in the plasma membrane helps in cellular recognition.

12. (D) The cell is the structural and functional unit of life.

13. (C) Plasma membrane or cell membrane does all the tasks mentioned in the question.

14. (B) Cytoplasm is divided into cytoplasm and nucleoplasm.

15. (A) The nucleus consists of genetic material in the form of a dense mass. It is surrounded by double membrane called nuclear envelope. It is the controlling centre of the cell.

16. (D) Nucleus contains thread-like structures called chromosomes which are visible in a cell in the resting stage as chromatin threads. These threads unwind, shorten and thicken during cell division to become chromosomes.

17. (B) RBC of mammals do not contain nucleus, brain cells contain single nucleus and a paramoecium contains two nuclei.

18. (A) Nucleus is called the 'control room' or 'brain' of the cell because it controls all the functions of the cell.

19. (A) Mitochondria are the sites of cell respiration.

20. (C) ATP is also called energy currency of the cell.

21. (D) Endoplasmic Reticulum(ER) is tubular in structure which helps in the transport of substances within the cell. It is also called as endoskeleton of the cell.

22. (D) Golgi body helps in the secretion of substances like enzymes, it helps in the proper metabolic functioning of the cell.

23. (C) Lysosomes are known as the digestive organs of the cell. They engulf food materials and other substances which are hydrolysed by enzymes.

24. (B) When cell becomes old or damaged beyond repair, the lysosmes secrete enzymes in the cytoplasm that leads to the death of the cell. Hence, they are called the suicide bags of the cell. The energy in the form of ATP is stored in mitochondria and hence are called the power house of the cell.

25. (C) Centrosome is an organelle present near the nucleus of an animal cell. It initiates the process of cell division. In plant cells, centrioles appear only at the time of cell division.

26. (D) Plastids are of three types, i.e. chloroplasts, leucoplasts and chromoplasts. Leucoplasts are colourless plastids which are capable of storing food materials.

27. (C) The green plastids present in plant cells are chloroplasts. Chloroplasts contain green coloured pigment called chlorophyll.

28. (C) The cell wall is made up of cellulose.

29. (B) Epithelial cells line the hollow organs and glands and also cover the whole surface of the body. They secrete a variety of chemicals and are involved in receiving external stimuli.

30. (D) Cell wall is the non - living part of the plant cell.

☞ **Previous Contest Questions**

1. (B) In the given options B represents endoplasmic reticulum. It helps in giving mechanical support and enzyme transportation.

2. (A) Golgi complex receives the substances synthesized and release by the ER, condenses, modifies, packs and releases them in the form of secretory vesicles.

3. (D) In the given options lysosomes do not contain DNA.

4. (D) Mitochondria - provides energy, chloroplast - helps in synthesis of food, nucleus - controls all the activities of the cell and cell wall - gives shape to the cell.

5. (A) Germinating seeds contain more mitochondria.

6. (B) The blood is a liquid connective tissue.

7. (A) In a cell the following organelles perform the following functions. Intracellular digestion - lysosome, intracellular respiration - mitochondira, intracellular movement - microtubules, cell secretion - golgi complex.

8. (D) Muscle tissues, eptithelial tissues and connective tissues are present in stomach.

9. (B) Nerve cells are branched structures.

10. (B) Onion peel cells are plant cells.

3. Microorganisms

☞ **Multiple Choice Questions**

1. (D) Virus is the smallest microorganism.

2. (C) In the given figure W - virus, X - fungus and Y - protozoan.

3. (B) Nutrition and respiration are the two factors that are taken to classify bacteria.

4. (B) Bacteriophage is a type of virus which attacks bacteria.

5. (D) Fungi reproduces by spore formation.

6. (B) Algae can manufacture their own food.

7. (B) The absence of light and moist temperature favour the growth of the fungus.

8. (B) Bacteria play an important role in maintaining the balance of nitrogen gas in the atmosphere.

9. (D) The release of carbon dioxide gas causes dough to rise when yeast is addded to it. (Fermentation)

10. (B) Fermentation takes place when yeast is added to grape juice and left for a week.

11. (B) Cellulase is secreted by bacteria that can digest cellulose.

12. (D) The production of hormones and gene therapy through micro-organism is taken up in the field of biotech-nology.

13. (D) Antibiotics cheese and yoghurt are produced by bacteria.

14. (C) The microorganisms that cause diseases are called pathogens.

15. (D) Pathogens causing Dengue fever and malaria are carried by mosquitoes.

16. (B) The disease is malaria.

17. (D) Options (i) and (ii) are true about the microorganisms the diseases they cause and the symptoms.

18. (C) Improving personal hygiene prevents ringworm disease.

19. (A) Rhizobium bacteria live symbiotically.

20. (D) Vibrio causes cholera.

21. (A) Cellulose is digested by bacteria living in the intestines of herbivorous animals.

22. (A) Penicillium notatum has given one of the greatest drugs to the world of medicine.

23. (A) Spirogyra is called pond silk.

24. (B) The characteristics features which distinguishes algae from fungi is autotrophic nutrition.

25. (C) Through contaminated food and water enters the human body.

26. (B) Viruses cause common cold.

27. (A) Viruses multiply only in living host suggests that viruses are living.

28. (D) Microorganisms are used in the production of antibiotics.

29. (C) X represents yeast cells are useful in preparing wine.

30. (D) The mode of transmission of infectious diseases is through body contact, air and a vector.

Explanatory Answers

Previous Contest Questions

1. (C) In the figure X represents viruses.

2. (A) Bacillus is the largest bacteria.

3. (C) Antibodies are produced by an organism to prevent or reduce the spread of microorganisms.

4. (A) Bacteria have an ability to help in recycling of nutrients and energy.

5. (D) Spirogyra differs from a paramoecium in having plastids.

6. (A) Options A is euglena which can prepare its own food.

7. (D) Fungi and bacteria are used in making antibiotics.

8. (B) P - Bacillus, Q - Coccus, R - Spirillum and S - Vibrio.

9. (A) Viruses cause dengue fever.

10. (A) Lichens exhibit symbiotic life.

4. Conservation of Plants and Animals

Multiple Choice Questions

1. (B) The diversity of genes, species and ecosystems of a region is called biodiversity.

2. (D) Uncontrolled deforestation leads to destruction of habitats, soil erosion, flash floods, increase of carbon dioxide in the air and global warming.

3. (C) Drought which is caused due to lack of rains results in decreased food production.

4. (A) Biosphere is the name given to the region that include all living organisms and all life supporting regions of the earth.

5. (B) By recycling resources, we can prevent overexploitation of resouces and conserve the resources and in turn conserve the environment.

6. (C) The non-living or abiotic components of an ecosystem are air, water, temperature, soil etc.

7. (D) Excess timber logging results in deforestation which causes flooding, soil erosion, etc. Selective logging(i.e the logging of only matured trees should be practised). Reforestation helps in minimising the effect of mismanagement.

8. (B) Conservation involves keeping the natural environment in its balanced state. Preservation involves keeping some of the earth's resources for future generations.

9. (C) The introduction of exotic species into an area disturbs the natural ecological balance. They compete with the native species for nutrients, shelter and spread new diseases.

10. (D) Forests stop soil erosion, provide shelter and thus prevent floods. Forests provide us with oxygen and rainfall.

11. (A) Shifting cultivation is practised by tribals where they clear a new forest area for cultivation and then move on to a new part after few seasons.

12. (D) IUCN red list is a book which keeps the record of all the endangered plants and animals.

13. (D) There are various projects taken up by the Government which have helped in restoring the wildlife. Ban on hunting and sale of products from wildlife, afforestation, declaring forests as reserved areas, establishing national parks and sanctuaries are the steps, helpful in restoring the wildlife.

14. (B) The root system of many plants especially grasses, have high soil binding capacity and thus help in the prevention of soil erosion.

15. (B) Deforestation causes soil erosion causes desertification and floods. It can be prevented by afforestation, proper land management and preventing overgrazing.

16. (B) Conservation helps to prevent extinction of endangered species.

17. (D) Plants known as flora and animals, fauna are living resources in nature.

18. (A) An animal on the verge of extinction is called an endangered animal.

19. (D) Habitat destruction, over use of natural resources and mans's interference with nature pose a threat to biodiversity.

20. (B) Biological imbalance is a consequence of man's interference with nature.

21. (A) National parks are areas strictly reserved for improvement of wild life and help in protecting wild animals especially the endangered species.

22. (C) Poaching that endanger animals is the result of the interference of man with nature.

23. (C) Species which are on the verge of entering the endangered category are called vulnerable species.

24. (D) Forests are biodiversity hot spots.

25. (B) Energy flow in an ecosystem is unidirectional.

26. (D) Rain water harvesting, conservation of oceans, preservation of marine and wild life can restore balance in an ecosystem.

27. (C) Human beings and their activities disturb the habitat of tigers.

28. (B) Green revolution is not the reason for the fall in biodiversity.

29. (C) Gene pool helps in maintaining diversity.

30. (B) Wildlife is commercially important. This renders choice B incorrect.

31. (D) Fox is not an endangered wild animal of India.

32. (A) All non - domesticated and non - cultivated biota found in their natural habitat is called wild life.

33. (A) Deccan plateau has rich flora and fauna.

34. (A) In 1972 Wildlife Protection Act was passed.

35. (C) Importing organisms from other countries is not an effective way to conserve living organisms.

☞ **Previous Contest Questions**

1. (D) Using animal parts as traditional medicines, encouraging game hunting as a sport, using animal parts as decorative pieces are human activities that may cause the extinction of a species.

2. (A) Endemic species are plants and animals that are exclusively found in a particular regions.

3. (B) Deforestation increases the carbon dioxide content in the atmosphere which results in the greenhouse effect.

4. (D) Conservation involves keeping the natural environment in its balanced state. Preservation involves keeping some of the earth's resources for future generations.

5. (D) The Karnataka government had launched "project elephant" to save Asian elephants in the state.

6. (D) For the preservation of a species, there should be a protected area for endangered plants and animals as well as protection of their breeding grounds.

7. (B) Under MAB programme, a core zone is an area where human activity is not permitted.

8. (D) Using earth's resources wisely, can help us to conserve natural resources.

9. (B) Swarming is the mass emigration of bees to settle down elsewhere in order to form a new hive.

10. (D) The proper management of the environment is important to maintain the balance nature so that both animals and man can continue to live.

5. Reproduction in Animals

☞ **Multiple Choice Questions**

1. (A) Reproduction without the fusion of gametes is known as asexual

reproduction. The offspring are genetically identical.

2. (D) In sexual reproduction, the offspring receives characteristics from both the parents. .

3. (D) Butterfly undergoes sexual reproduction..

4. (D) Ovaries testes and fallopian tubes are the paired structures in human reproductive system.

5. (D) An egg cell can live in the body for only one day.

6. (A) W is placenta, X is foetal, Y is amniotic fluid and Z is foetal membrane.

7. (C) Placenta prevents the mixing of the blood of the foetus with that of the mother.

8. (A) The correct sequence in the formation of a baby is as follows.

   Zygote → Embryo → Foetus → Baby

9. (A) All living organisms reproduce.

10. (A) Hydra reproduces by budding.

11. (D) Budding, binary fission, spore formation are types of asexual reproduction.

12. (B) Options I and III are true of comparison of sexual and asexual reproduction.

13. (D) Unicellular organisms like amoeba and paramoecium undergoes binary fission.

14. (D) Fertilisation takes place in the fallopian tube.

15. (C) R - ovulation, S - implantation and T - fertilization.

16. (A) P is ovulation, Q is implantation and R is fertilization.

17. (C) The fluid protects the foetus from shock.

18. (D) Umbilical cord transports urea, antibodies and carbon dioxide.

19. (C) R represents pupa.

20. (D) Fertilisation is external in fish and amphibians.

21. (A) Two daughter cells are formed as a result of binary fission.

22. (B) The larva of a frog is tadpole.

23. (C) The casting off of the skin by a caterpillar to allow a larger caterpillar to emerge is called moulting.

24. (A) The correct route the sperm takes after leaving the testis is epididymis - vas deferens - ejaculatory duct - urethra.

25. (C) The fallopian tubes have an internal wall lined with fingerlike projections.

26. (C) Testes contain seminiferous tubules.

27. (B) Sperms mature in epididymis.

28. (A) Ovum is released during ovulation.

29. (D) Uterus is an unpaired structure.

30. (A) Options A is the correct statement.

31. (B) Placenta is a specialised structure that provides nourishment to the foetus from the mother and collects wastes from it, passing them onto the mother.

32. (D) Oxygen and amino acids are found in high concentrations in the blood that passes from the placenta to the foetus.

33. (B) The function of the secretions of cowpers gland is to serve as a lubricant.

34. (A) Protozoa reproduces asexually.

35. (D) AIDS is a deadly disease caused by a virus.

☞ **Previous Contest Questions**

1. (B) Frogs have ampluxory pads that help in copulation.

2. (C) Spermatozoa are present in the milt of frog.

3. (D) Statements II and III are true.

   Menstruation occurs every 28 days and during every menstrual cycle, one mature ovum will be released by the ovary.

4. (C) Placenta in the uterus prevents the mixing of the blood of the foetus with

Explanatory Answers

that of the mother.

5. (A) Echidna is an oviparous mammal.

6. (B) The given figure represents fertilisation.

7. (C) The mass of eggs of a frog is called spawn.

8. (D) Internal fertilization occurs in snakes and rabbits.

9. (D) Ovary has graafian follicles.

10. (D) One ova is released at a time in female human beings.

6. Reaching the Age of Adolescence

☞ **Multiple Choice Questions**

1. (B) Girls reach puberty earlier than boys. In girls, adolescence may begin a year or two earlier than in boys.

2. (B) Growth is the process in which the size of an individual increases permanently from the zygote stage to the adult stage. The first three years is the infancy period, followed by childhood. Adolescence begins around the age 11 and lasts upto 18 or 19 years of age.

3. (C) The period after childhood is that of the adolescence. It begins around the age of 11 and lasts upto 18 or 19 years of age.

4. (A) Growth takes place by cell division. During infancy growth rate is very fast. Growth slows down during childhood(3-11 years) and during adolescence very rapid growth occurs.

5. (D) At the beginning of adulthood, the growth is maximum.

6. (B) The testes produce male gametes called sperms which fertilise the egg to form a zygote.

7. (D) Hormones are chemical substances. The changes which occur at adolescence are controlled by hormones. Testosterone is the male hormone. Oestrogen and progesterone are the female hormones.

8. (D) The onset of puberty brings about the growth of the reproductive organs. In girls, production of egg cells and menstruation, growth of pubic hair and armpit hair, enlargement of breasts and buttocks takeplace during adolescence.

9. (B) The release of the egg cell is called ovulation. During menstrual cycle, 13th to 15th day after menstruation, an egg cell is most likely to be released from an ovary.

10. (B) Girls reach puberty earlier than boys and they overtake boys in height during adolescence.

11. (B) The human body undergoes several changes during adolescence. These changes mark the onset of puberty. During puberty, secondary sexual characteristics develop. Girls reach puberty earlier than boys.

12. (B) Adolescence is a stage of rapid growth and development. Hence, a balanced diet rich in proteins is essential.

13. (B) Deepening of voice is a secondary sexual characteristic of a boy.

14. (D) During puberty, physical and emotional changes take place in the adolescents. These changes are called secondary sexual characteristics.

15. (B) During menopause, the menstrual cycle stops. It is likely to occur when a woman is about 45 to 50 years old.

16. (C) Repair and growth of the uterine lining and ovulation does not take place during the final stage of menstrual cycle.

17. (A) Adrenaline hormone is secreted by the adrenal cortex of kidney.

18. (B) Iodine is essential for the efficient functioning of thyroid gland.

19. (D) The changes which occur at adolescence are controlled by sex hormones. The male hormone or testosterone controls the development of male secondary sexual characteristics.

20. (A) Thyroxine is secreted by the thyroid gland. Metamorphosis in insects is

Explanatory Answers

controlled by thyroxine.

21. (B) Chromosomes concerned with sex are called allosomes or sex chromosomes. They are XX in female and XY in male.

22. (B) In our country, the legal age for marriage is 18 years for girls and 21 years for boys.

23. (D) Pituitary gland is also known as the master gland as it controls other endocrine glands.

24. (D) Ovaries secrete hormones such as oestrogen and progesterone, which controls the different phases of the menstrual cycle.

25. (B) Hormones are secreted in small quantities directly into the bloodstream.

☞ **Previous Contest Questions**

1. (C) Hyposecretion of insulin hormone by pancreas leads to diabetes mellitus.

2. (A) Fertilization is the process during which a sperm fuses with an egg cell to form a zygote.

3. (B) Sex of the offspring in humans is determined by father's sex chromosomes.

4. (A) The correct sequence of the stages of growth is : zygote, embryo, foetus, baby, child, adolescent, adult.

5. (B) The correct sequence of the menstrual cycle follows is the uterus wall thickness with blood vessels, the ovary discharges an ovum, the ovum dies within 24 hours after ovulation and the uterus wall breaks down.

6. (D) In the figure X is testes, Y is ovum and Z is fertilization.

7. (D) Sertoli cells of testes secretes testosterone.

8. (C) Thymus gland is nearest to the heart.

9. (D) 44 + XX represents the composition of femaledestined zygote in human beings.

10. (C) Tears does not transmit HIV.

Questions@stimulating-minds

1. As half of the tank is filled with water that has a definite volume of 1500 cm³, the other half will be filled with air that takes up the other 1500 cm³. Air has no definite volume and no definite shape. The 600 cm³ of air pumped in will spread out to occupy the remaining space in the tank.

2. The average surface area of a human body is around 20000 cm². This means that the force acting on our body is around 200000 N. We are not aware of this external pressure as our internal body pressure is only slightly more than this air pressure.

3. Frictional force does not depend on the surface area of contact. It depends on the weight of an object. The heavier the object, the larger the frictional force. Therefore, it is easier to move a lighter object than a heavier object that is placed on the same type of surface.

4. The following three ways help a cyclist in a race to reduce air friction to the minimum:

   (i) Wear a smooth and tight-fitting suit.

   (ii) Ride a streamlined bicycle by wearing streamlined helmet and shoes.

   (iii) Base down to reduce the effects of air resistance.

5. An air-puck moves smoothly on a table because the layer of air between it and the top of the table reduces friction.

6. Stereophonic hearing refers to hearing with two ears. Stereophonic hearing enables us to determine the direction of sound accurately.

   (a) The ear closer to the source of the sound receives the sound slightly earlier and louder than the other ear.

   (b) The brain interprets these differences and enables us to determine the location of the source of the sound.

   (c) A person with only one ear functioning cannot determine the direction of sounds accurately.

7. The image formed in the eye is accurate but the brain sometimes cannot interpret it accurately. This gives rise to optical illusions.

Sometimes what we see is different from reality. What we see depends not only on our eyes, but also our brain as shown below.

AB appears longer than CD. Both are actually equal in length.

Lines E and F appear bent. they are actually straight.

Most people see a curvy line eventhough none is drawn.

8. Our sense of sight has its limitations. For example.

   (a) We cannot see very tiny objects such as microorganisms and atoms with the naked eye.

   (b) We cannot see very distant objects such as the stars and the planets.

   (c) We cannot see the bones and organs inside our body. This is because we cannot see through opaque objects.

9. Stars are classified based on their colour and temperature as shown below.

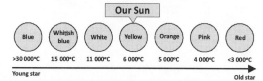

10. The polymerisation reaction involves breaking the carbon-carbon bond to form a new carbon-carbon bond between ethene molecules. This reaction requires high energy and a catalyst helps to provide an alternate pathway with a lower energy.

11. Silver, gold and platinum are not reactive with oxygen and water. These are stable metals and they can be worn as jewellery. Iron reacts with oxygen and water and forms rust.

12. Aluminium forms a very thin layer of aluminium oxide on its surface when exposed to air. This layer protects it form further atmospheric corrosion and makes it less reactive chemically.

13. Natural gas occupies 600 times less volume as a liquid than as a gas.

14. Petrol is less dense than water. So, when water is sprayed on a fire caused by petrol, the petrol will float on water and continues burning.

15. The redox reactions in catalytic converters produce CO_2 which is a green house gas which may contribute to global warming.

16. Water purified by passing chlorine gas into water to kill micro-organisms has pungent odour. In order to make the water free from this odour, ozone is widely used in water purification plants. Ozone has no taste, smell like chlorine, and no harmful by products are formed. It does not irritate our skin or eyes but can kill micro-organisms in water.

17. No. These outfits restrict movements and not very comfortable to be worn everyday.

18. The scrubber is an apparatus consisting of a tank spraying water at the smoke before allowing it into the exhaust pipe. Water will dissolve the poisonous gases and particles in the smoke before it is discharged as shown below.

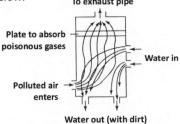

To exhaust pipe
Plate to absorb poisonous gases
Water in
Polluted air enters
Water out (with dirt)

It is used in factories and power stations to clean the smoke emissions before discharging it into the atmosphere.

19. Primitive humans were wandering food gatherers. They ate raw fruits and vegetables and hunted animals for food.

20. Tilled soil may have big lumps of soil. These need to be crushed and the soil should be levelled. This is done with the help of a wooden or iron leveller. Levelling also prevents erosion of soil by wind or water.

21. Wheat crop does not require much water to grow, so wheat would not grow in kharif season. The seeds would get destroyed in excess water due to rainy season.

22. Viruses are very small infectious agents. Inside a host cell, they multiply and reproduce to form a number of viruses. During their multiplication, they cause diseases in host organisms. They have their own genetic material thus they resemble living organisms. But outside the host cell, they behave like a non-living particle. They cannot multiply outside host cell and lack cellular structure. As they resemble both living and non-living being thus they are considered to be on the borderline of living and non-living.

23. Arctic tern.

24. If we go on cutting trees then ecological balance will be disturbed. Earth will loose top fertile layer and will be converted into desert. Floods and droughts will become more frequent. Many animals will lose their shelters. There will be scarcity of things like fruits, paper, wood which we get from forests. Global warming will occur.

25. The wood pulp is used in manufacturing the papers. It takes 17 full grown trees to make one tonne of paper. So, we should save paper to protect our trees.

26. The size of the cells has no relation with the size of the body of the animal. It is not necessary that the cells in the elephant be much bigger than those in a rat. The size of the cell is related to its function.

27. When a cell is kept in a medium containing salt solution, water in the cell will move out of the cell and the cell will shrink. It is called exosmosis.

28. In addition to the cell membrane, there is an outer thick layer in cells of plants called cell wall. This additional layer surrounding the cell membrane is required by plants for protection. Plant cells need protection against variations in temperature, high wind speed, atmospheric moisture, etc. They are exposed to these variations because they cannot move.

29. The cells of leaf contain green coloured plastids called chloroplasts. These contain green pigment called chlorophyll. So, a leaf appears green.

30. The period between fertilisation and the birth of the baby is called gestation.

31. Brooding is the process in which birds provide warmth to the eggs to develop by sitting over them.

32. The baby sheep Dolly was developed from a cell taken from the mammary gland of a female sheep (Finn Dorsett Sheep), and an unfertilized egg taken from another female sheep (Scottish Blackface Ewe). The nucleus of the unfertilised egg was removed from it. Therefore, no chromosome (and hence no genes) remained in the egg shell. The two cells were then fused together. It started developing into an embryo. Then embryo was put inside the uterus of a Scottish Blackface Ewe. It developed into a baby sheep Dolly.

33. In oviparous animals such as butterfly and frog, the young ones that hatch out from the eggs look very different from the adult. They are called larvae. Metamorphosis is the process of transformation of larva in an adult through drastic changes. The process of a child changing into an adult cannot be called metamorphosis because the child resembles its parents at the time of birth.

34. Though fish and frogs lay hundreds of eggs all the eggs do not get fertilized and develop into new individuals. This is because the eggs get exposed to water movement, wind and rainfall. Also, there are other animals in the pond which may feed on eggs. Thus, production of large number of eggs is necessary to ensure fertilsation of at least a few of them.

35. Cats produce more than one egg at a time. All these eggs get fertilised and hence more than one babies are born to them at the same time. On the contrary human female produce only one egg at a time thus normally only one baby at a time.

36. During adolescent period, both sweat glands and sebaceous glands become more active specially on the face. This leads to appearance of acne and pimples on the face.

37. In boys, at puberty, the voice box or larynx protrudes out in the throat region as Adam's apple.

38. Sex hormones are the hormones secreted by testes (testosterone) and ovaries (estrogen). They are called sex hormones. Their function is to develop the secondary sexual characters in boys and girls.

CROSSWORD SOLUTIONS

1. Force and Pressure

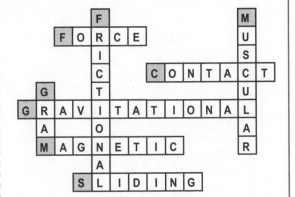

2. Friction

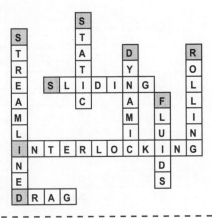

3. Sound

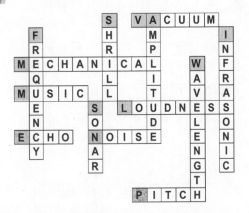

4. Chemical Effects of Electric Current

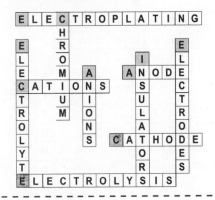

5. Some Natural Phenomena

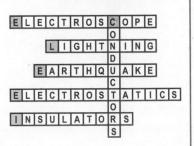

6. Light

7. Stars and The Solar System

CROSSWORD SOLUTIONS

1. Synthetic Fibres and Plastics

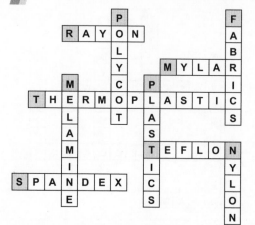

2. Materials : Metals and Non-metals

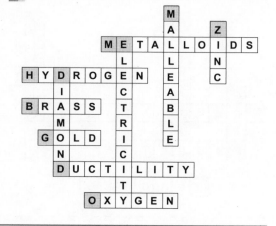

3. Coal and Petroleum

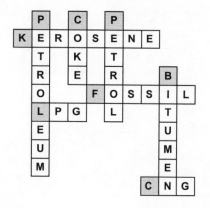

4. Combustion and Flame

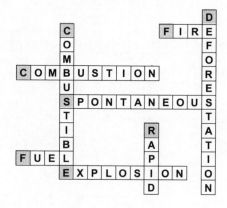

5. Pollution of Air and Water

CROSSWORD SOLUTIONS

1. Food Production and Management

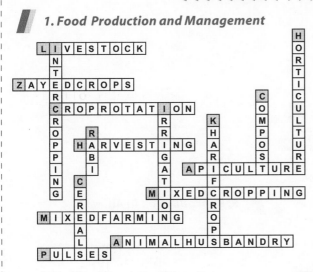

2. Cell

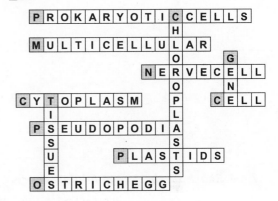

3. Microorganisms

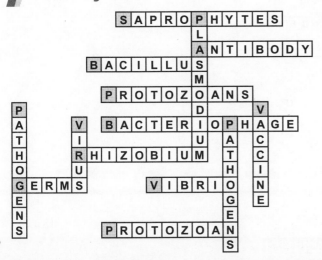

4. Conservation of Plants and Animals

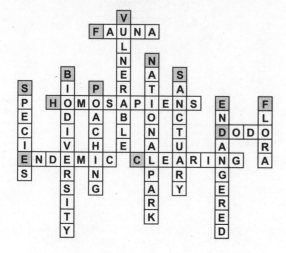

5. Reproduction in Animals

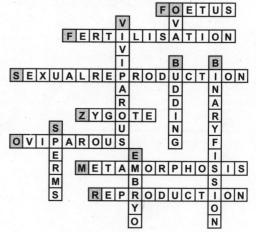

6. Reaching the Age of Adolescenece

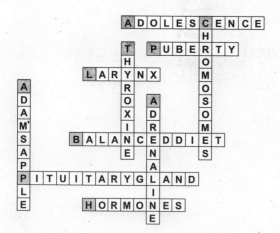